Contents

CB135010

Topic 1 What English do I know?

1 Trace and write. 2

1  one teacher  three teachers

2  one boy  four boys

3  one girl  two ....

4  one student  five ....

Numbers

one	six
two	seven
three	eight
four	nine
five	ten

People

boy	student
girl	teacher

2 Trace and match.

one
two
three
four
five

7 2 8 3 1 6 4 10 5 9

six
seven
eight
nine
ten

We're students.

I'm a teacher.
You're a student.
He's a boy.
She's a girl.
We're a class.

1 Listen and write. 3

He's
She's

1

2

.... a teacher.

.... a girl.

3

4

.... a teacher.

.... a boy.

2 Look, read and match.

I'm a student.

We're students.

You're a student.

1

2

3

1 Count and match.

1

2

3

4

5

a three boys

b one boy

c two girls

d six teachers

e five students

f four students and one teacher

g nine teachers

h ten students and one teacher

i seven students and one teacher

j eight girls

6

7

8

9

10

Listen and check. 4

1 Read and match.

1 He's a boy. He's three.

2 She's a girl. She's four.

3 She's a girl. She's five.

2 Read and write.

boy   girl   He's   She's

1

She's a ....

.... seven.

2

.... a boy.

He's eight.

3

He's a ....

.... ten.

✧ **Draw the candles on the cakes.**

3 Listen and write. 🔊5

1

Happy birthday!

.... one.

2

It's our birthday.

.... six.

3

It's my birthday.

.... nine.

1 Trace.

1 two boys

2 two teachers

3 three girls

4 five students

✧ **Count and match.**

2 Read and write.

I'm
She's
We're
You're

1

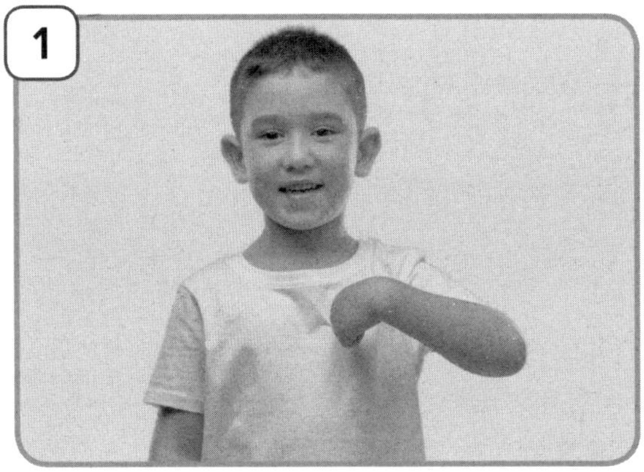

.... a student.

2

.... a student.

3

.... students.

4

.... a teacher.

✧ **Listen and check.** 6

1 Write the numbers.

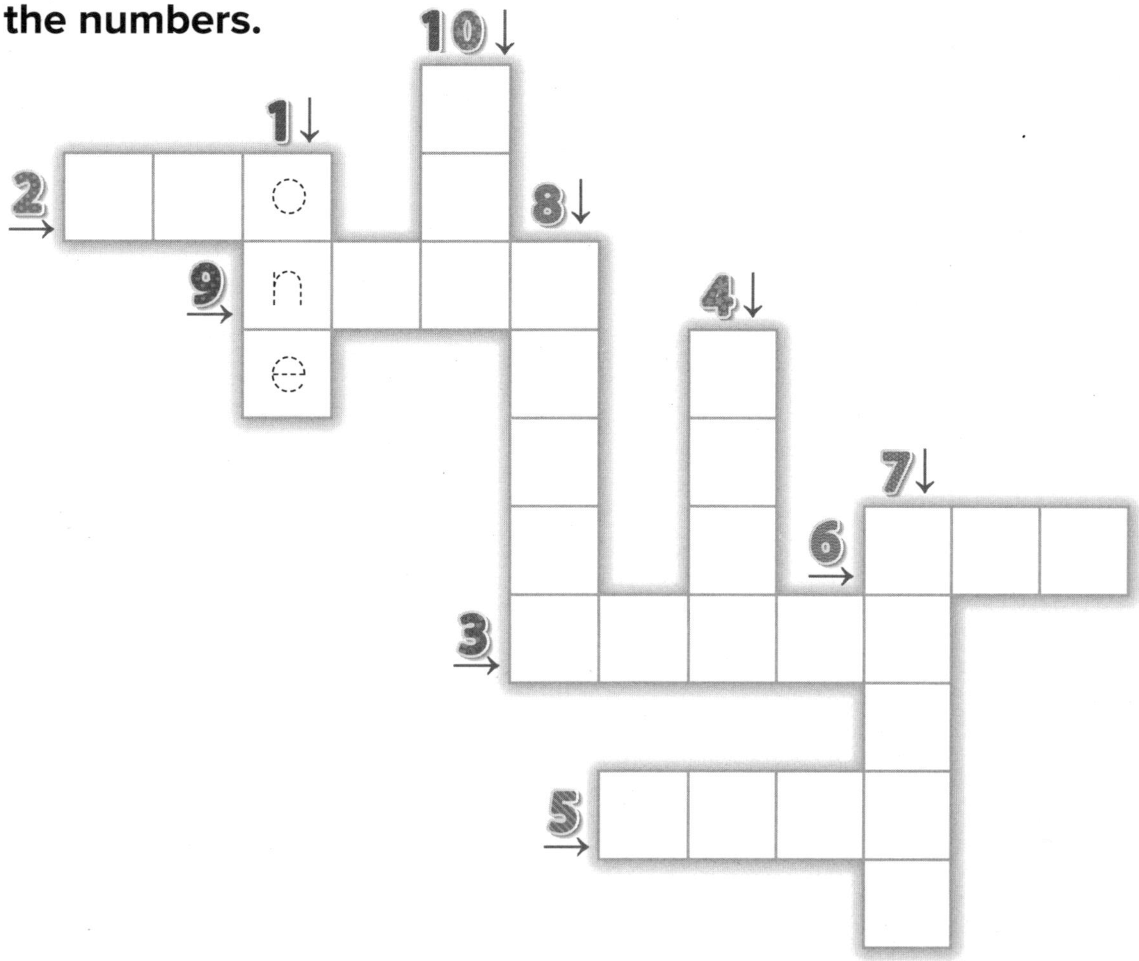

2 Look and unscramble the words.

1 lirg .... (7)

2 riach .... (4, 5, 3)

3 keds .... (2)

4 plicen .... (6)

5 duntset .... (1)

✧ Write the letters. Find the mystery word.

1	2	3	4	5	6	7

1 Look, read and circle.

1 a "We're teachers."

b "We're students."

c "We're boys."

2 Count! One, two, ...

a six. b nine. c three.

3 She's...

a a teacher. b a girl. c a boy.

4 Happy birthday! She's...

a seven. b eight. c six.

5 She ... a teacher.

a is b are c am

6 "We ... girls."

a am b is c are

7 "I ... a boy."

a am b are c is

8 "You ... a girl."

a am b is c are

2 Read again and check your answers.

1 Read and color.

1 Two books are red.
2 Two books are blue.
3 Three books are yellow.
4 One book is purple.

Colors
blue
green
orange
purple
red
yellow

Classroom Objects
book
chair
desk
pen
pencil

2 Label.

chair desk pen pencils

1 

....

2 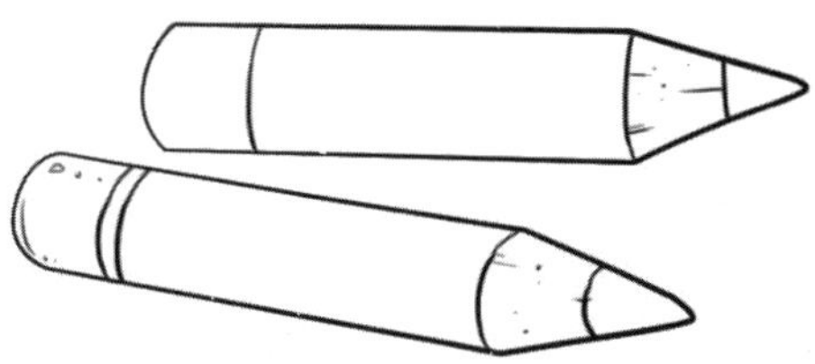

....

3 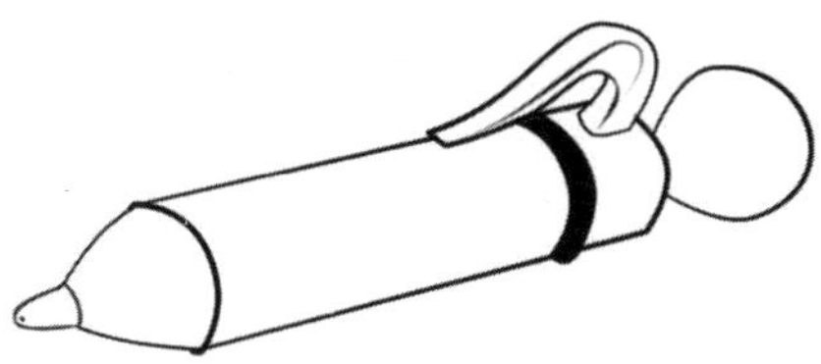

....

4 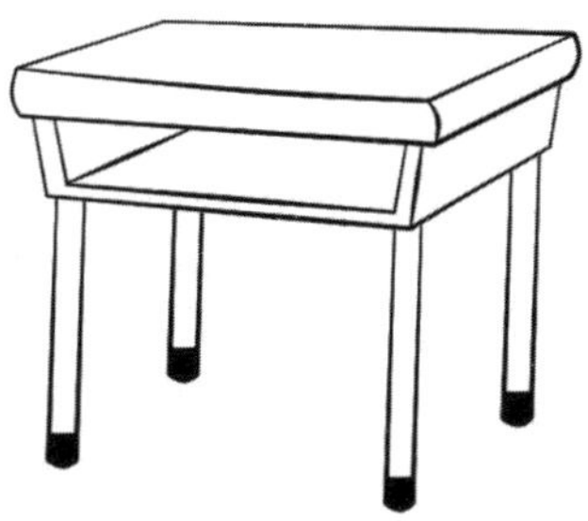

....

✧ Listen and color. 7

What is it?

What **is it**?
It's a book.
What color **is it**?
It's red.

What **are they**?
They're pens.
What color **are they**?
They're red.

1 Look, read and circle.

1 What is it?

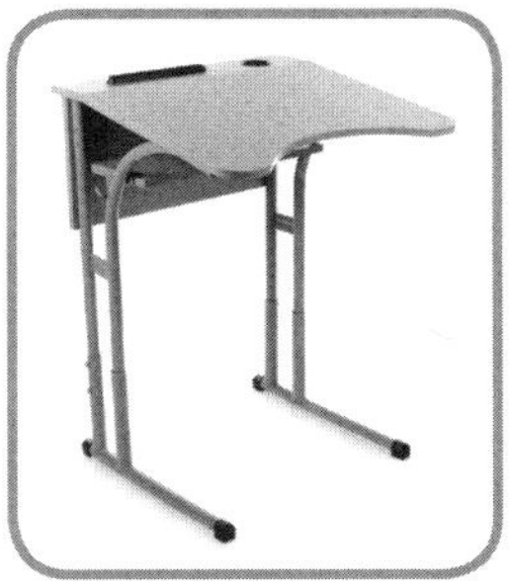

a It's a pen.
b They're desks.
c It's a desk.

2 What is it?

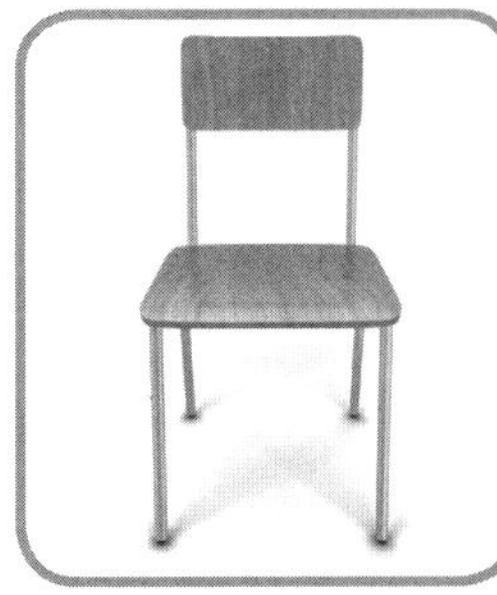

a They're books.
b It's a chair.
c It's a desk.

3 What are they?

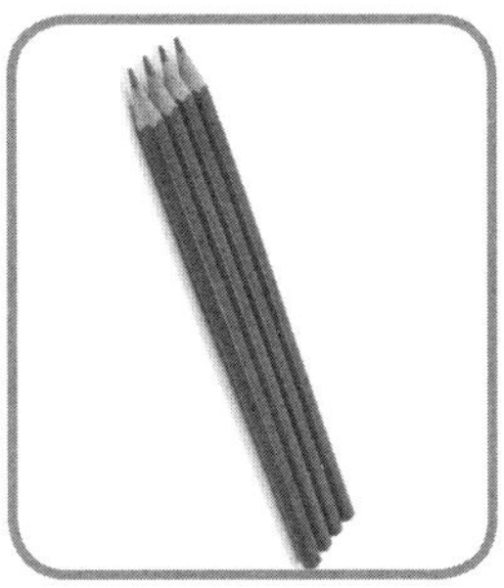

a They're chairs.
b They're pencils.
c It's a pencil.

4 What are they?

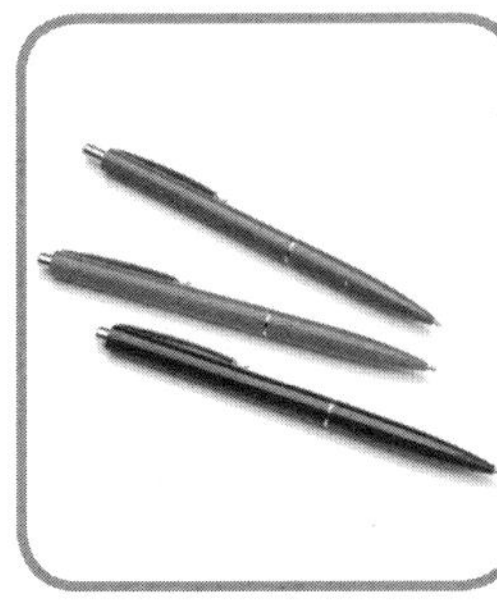

a It's a pen.
b They're books.
c They're pens.

2 Listen and number. 8

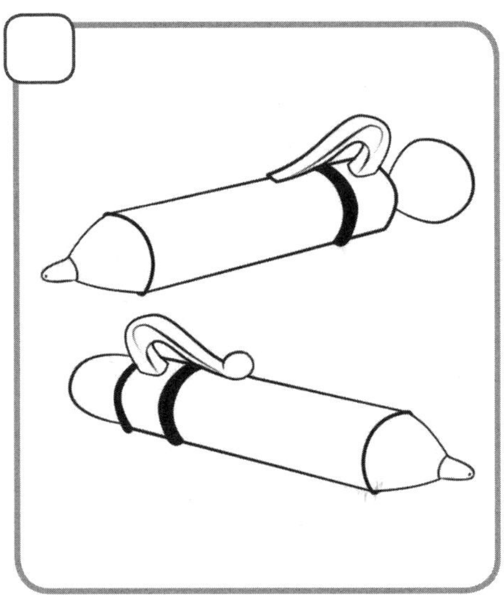

✧ **Listen again and color.**

1 Trace the questions.

What is it?

It's a **pencil / pen.**

What are they?

They're **pencils / pens.**

✧ Look and choose the answers.

2 Complete the questions.

are is it they

1 What .... it?

2 What color is ....?

3 What .... they?

4 What color are ....?

a It's yellow.

b They're purple.

c It's a chair.

d They're books.

✧ Match the questions with the answers.

1 Unscramble the questions.

1

is / What / it

....?

It's a ....

k o b o

2

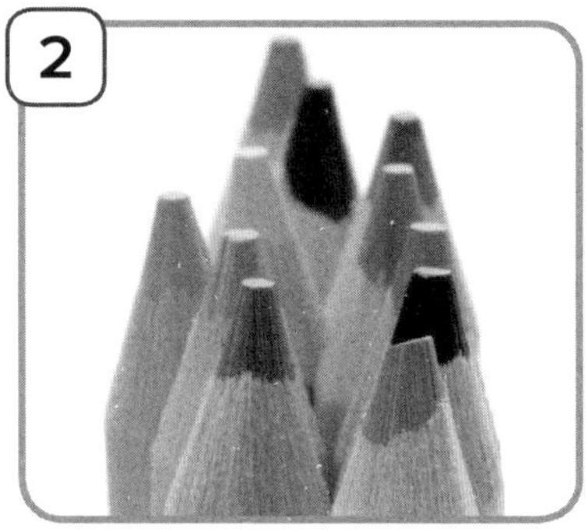

are / they / What

....?

They're ....

s l i c e n p

✧ **Look. Unscramble the answers.**

2 Answer the questions. Write and trace.

1

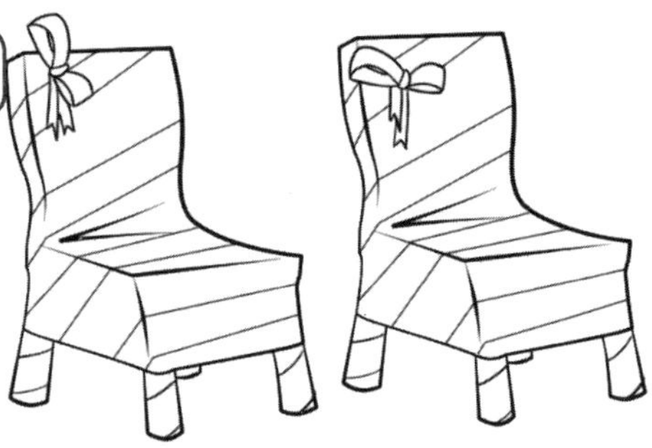

What are they?

.... chairs.

2

What is it?

.... a book.

3

What is it?

.... a desk.

1 Listen and circle. 9

1 What is it?

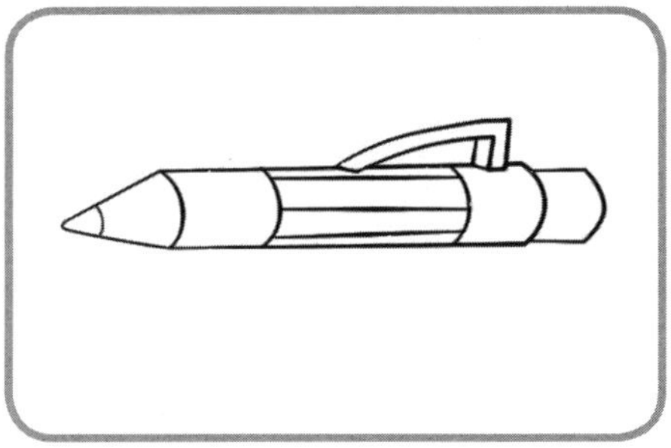

a It's a pen.

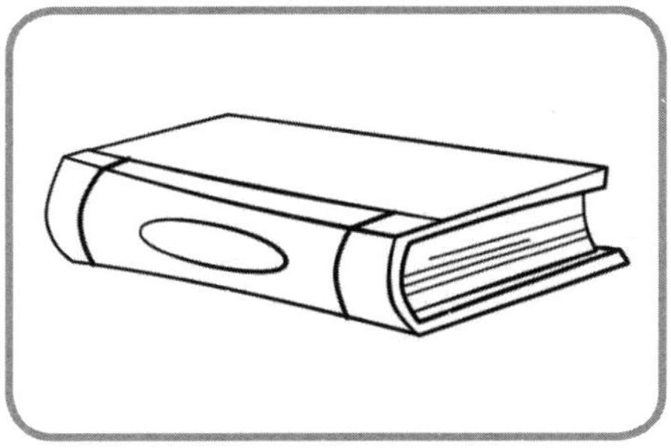

b It's a book.

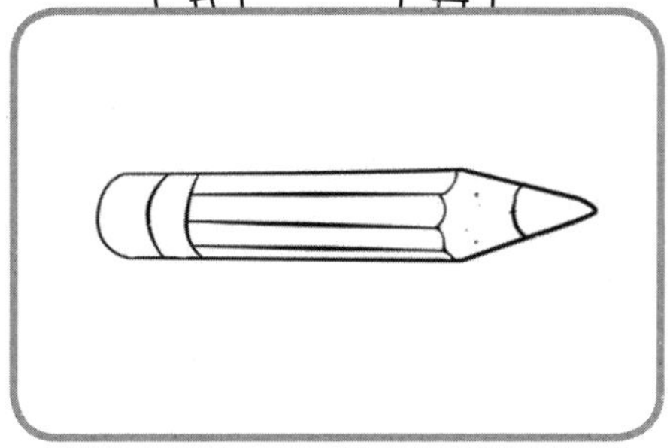

c It's a pencil.

2 What are they?

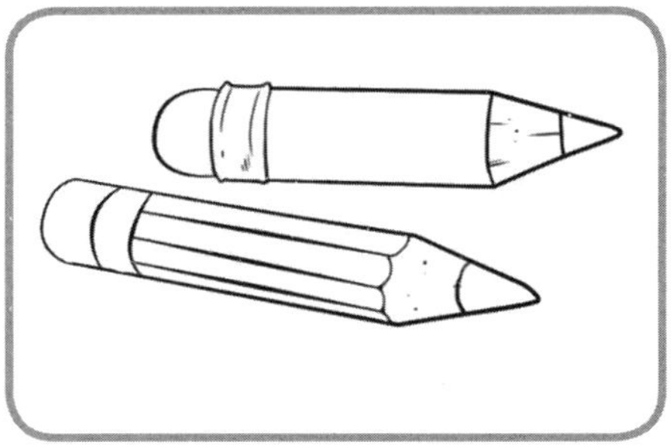

a They're pencils.

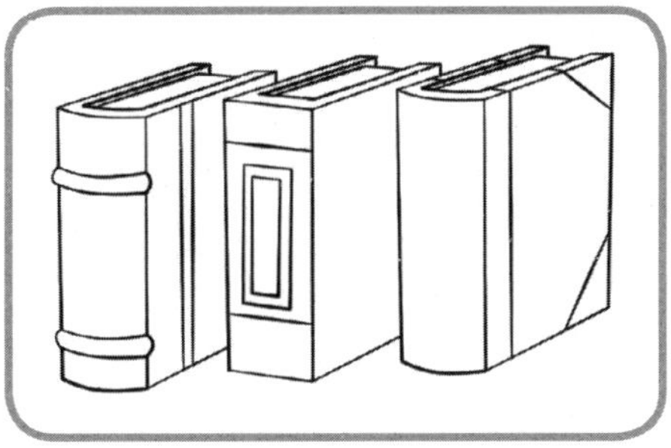

b They're books.

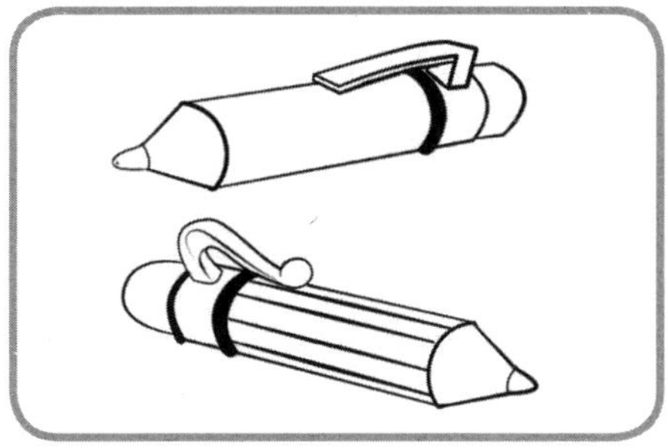

c They're pens.

Listen again and color.

2 Read, draw and color.

1

What is it?

It's a pencil.

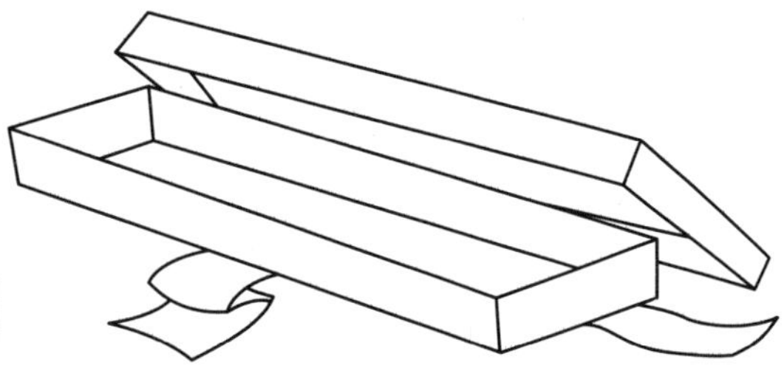

What color is it?

It's yellow and orange.

2

What are they?

They're pens. One, two, three!

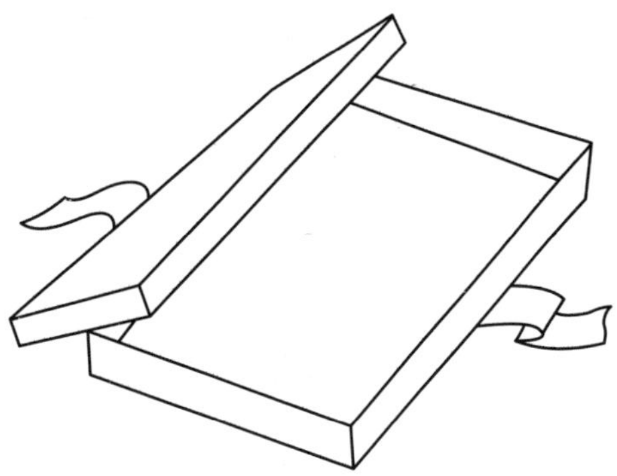

What color are they?

They're purple.

1 Circle the colors.

purpleredyellowgreenblueorange

2 Read the code. Color the classroom objects.

one = orange	two = blue	three = green
four = yellow	five = red	six = purple

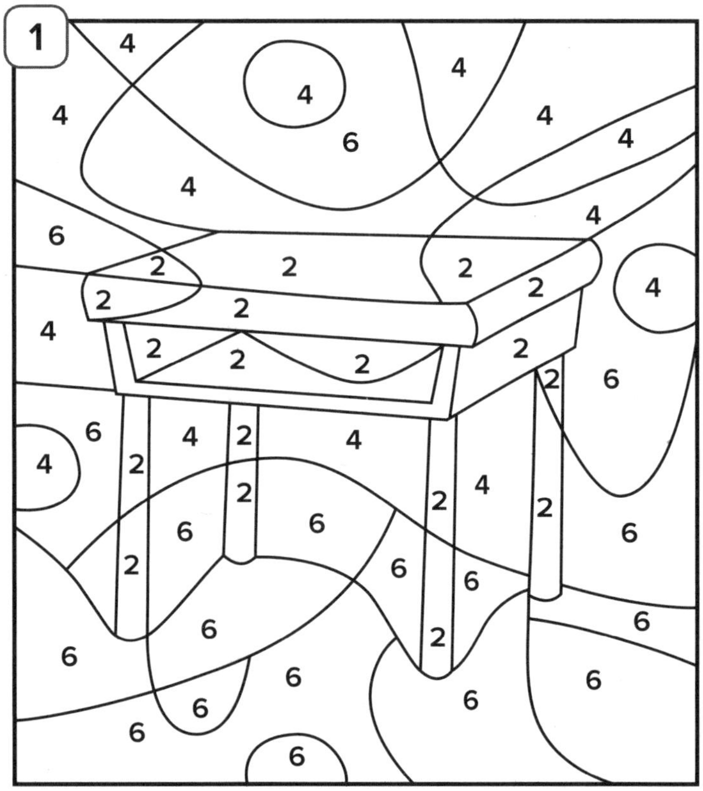

What is it?

It's a ....

What color is it?

It's ....

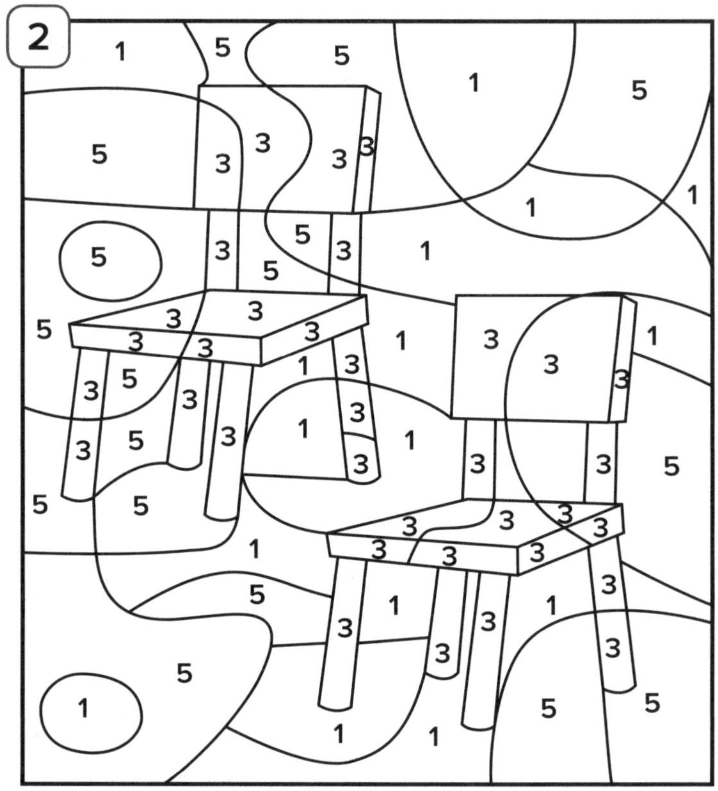

What are they?

....

What color are they?

....

✧ **Look and answer.**

1 Look, read and circle.

1 What are they?

a They're books.

b They're pens.

c They're pencils.

2 "What ... it?" "It's a rainbow."

a is b are c they

3 "What color ...?" "Lots of colors!"

a it is b are they c is it

4 a They're pens.

b They're pencils.

c It's a ruler.

5 a It's a book.

b They're books.

c It's a pencil.

6 a It's a desk.

b It's a chair.

c They're desks.

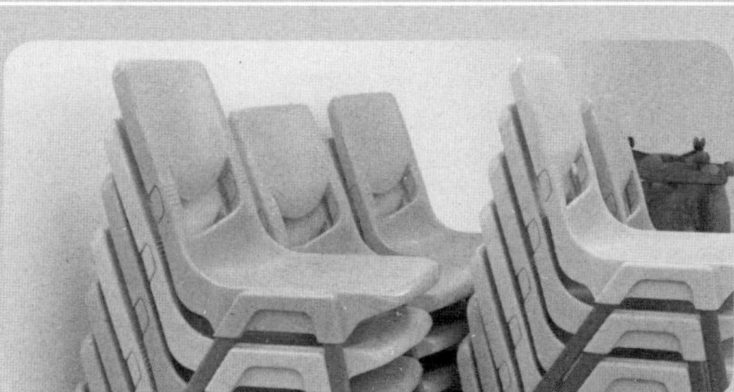

7 What ... they?

a are b is c it

8 They ... chairs.

a are b 's c is

2 Read again and check your answers.

Topic 2 What's in my school?

Classroom Objects

backpack
board
box
computer
eraser
ruler

Places

bathroom
classroom

1 Trace.

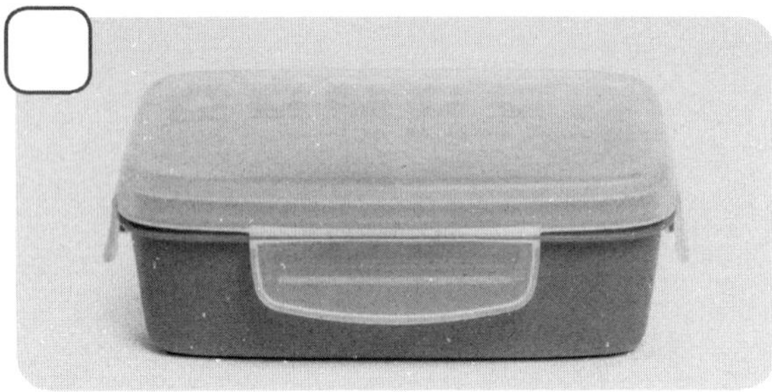

box

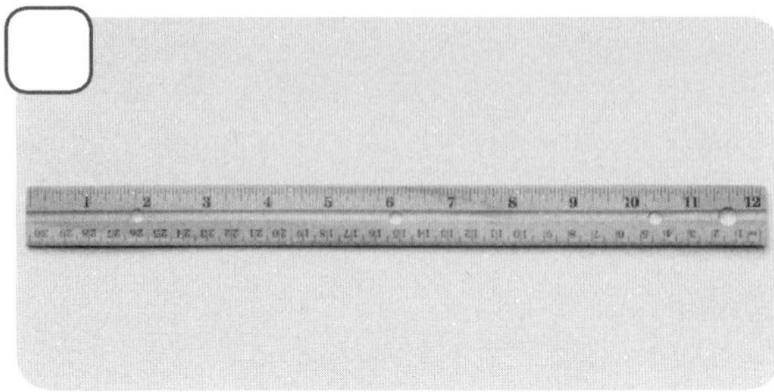

ruler

board

computer

eraser

backpack

bathroom

classroom

✧ **Listen and number.** 10

Where's my backpack?

Where's my backpack?

It's under the chair.

Where are my pencils?

They're on the desk.

Where's my ruler?

It's next to the computer.

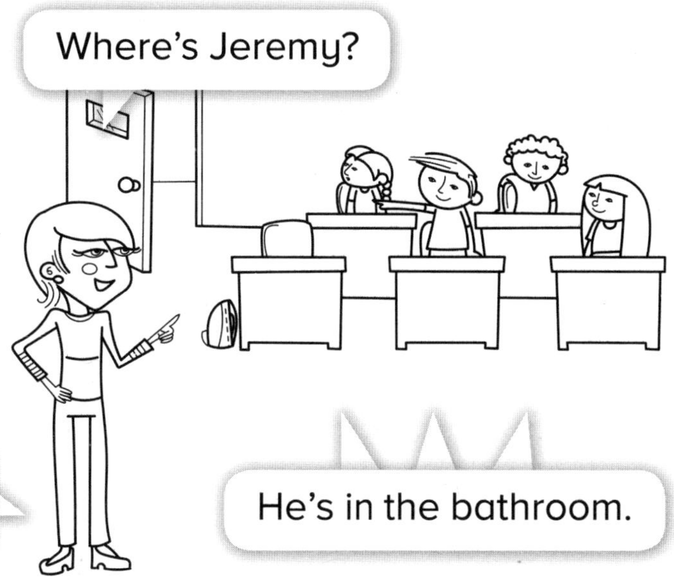

1 Look, read and match.

1 Where's my backpack?

2 Where are my books?

3 Where are my pens?

4 Where's my eraser?

5 Where are my students?

a They're on your chair.

b It's next to the board.

c It's next to the desk.

d They're in the bathroom!

e They're in your backpack.

Listen and check. 11

1 Listen and number the questions in order. 12

☐	Where's your book?	a	It's in my book.
☐	Where's your ruler?	b	It's in my backpack.
☐	Where's your box?	c	It's next to my box.
☐	Where's your backpack?	d	It's under my desk.

✧ **Listen again and match.**

✧ **Look and complete.**

next to   on   under

1 The computer is .... the teacher's desk.

2 The eraser is .... the computer.

3 The board is .... the teacher's desk.

4 The pens are .... the board.

1 Look, read and write *A* or *B*.

A

B

1 The books are under the desk. ☐

2 The books are on the desk. ☐

3 The pencils are under the chair. ☐

4 The pencils are under the desk. ☐

5 The crayon box is next to the computer. ☐

6 The crayon box is on the computer. ☐

7 The pens are under the desk. ☐

8 The pens are on the chair. ☐

9 The ruler is on the chair. ☐

10 The ruler is next to the chair. ☐

✧ Read and color.

1 The books under the desk are blue, orange and red.

2 The books on the desk are purple, green and yellow.

1 Unscramble the questions.

1 the computer / Where's

....? It's .... the desk.

2 are / the books / Where

....? They're .... the box.

3 Where's / the eraser

....? It's .... the box.

4 the ruler / Where's

....? It's .... the box.

✧ Listen and check. Complete the answers. 13

in   next to   on   under

✧ Read and draw.

1 **Trace a path from the classroom to the bathroom. Follow the classroom objects.**

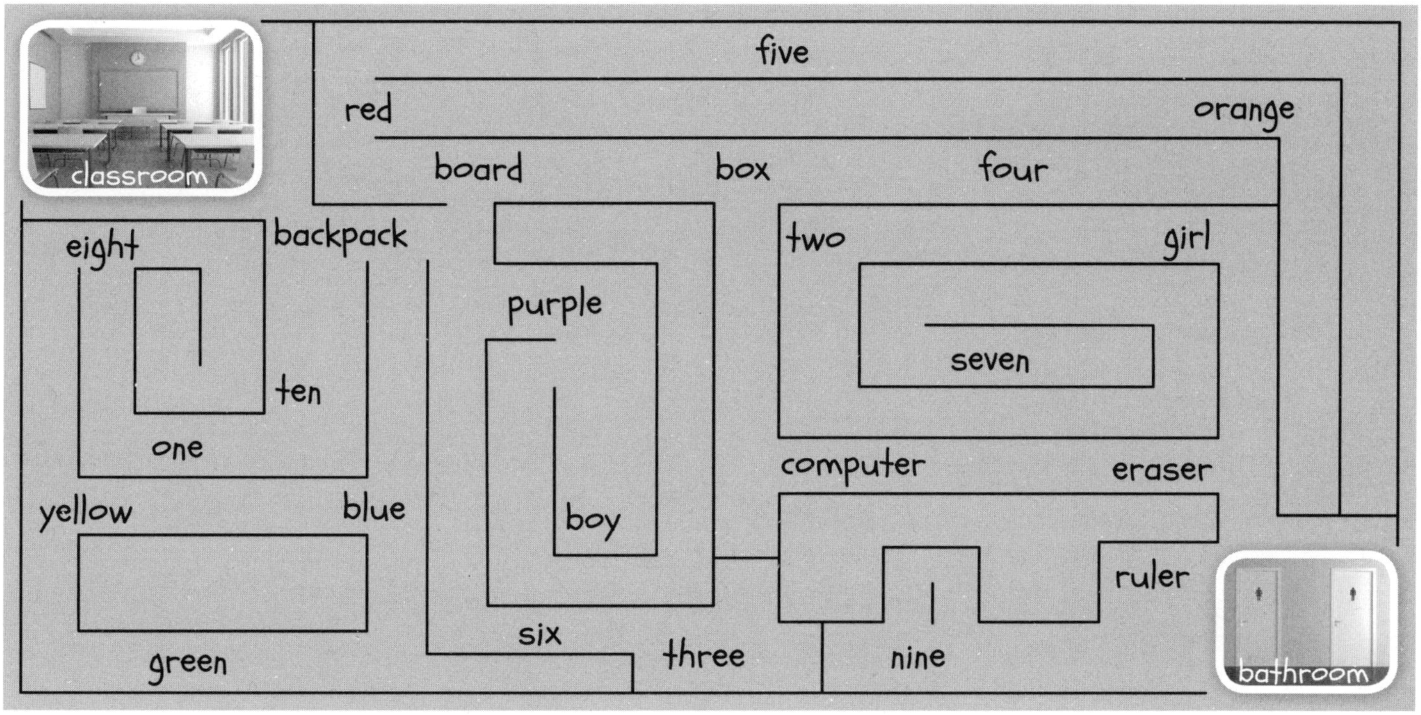

2 **Look and write the classroom objects.**

Across

1 

4 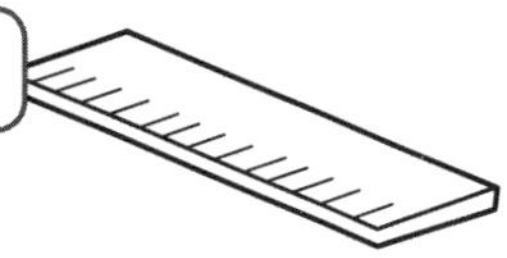

5 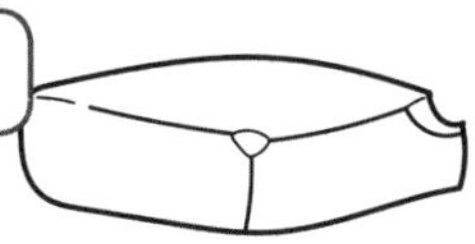

Down

1 

2 

3 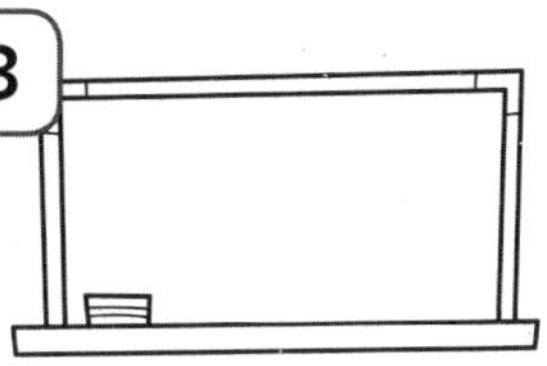

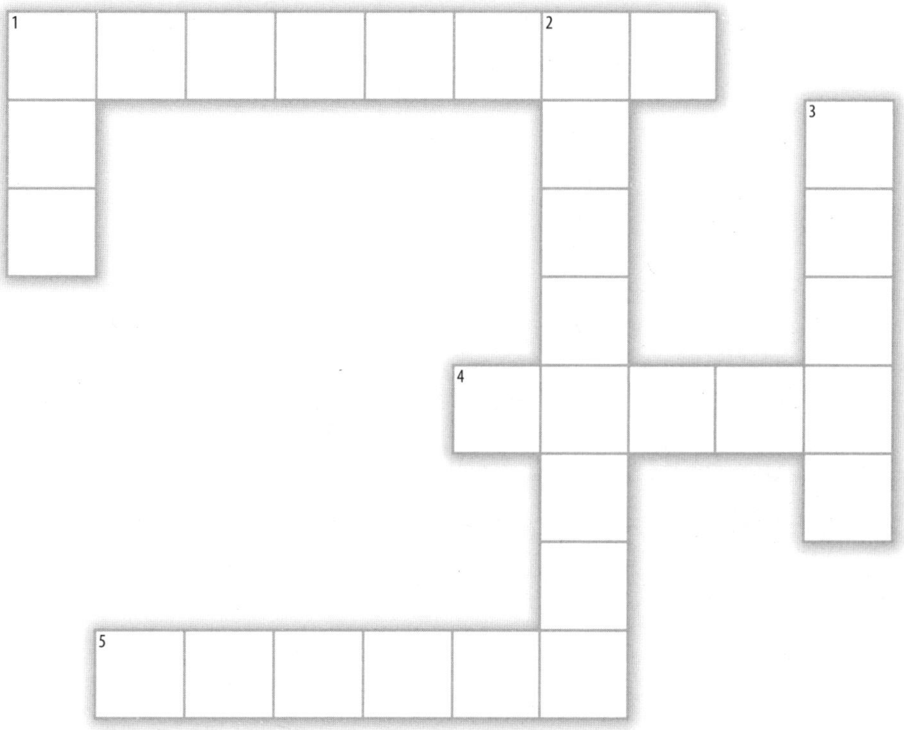

1 Look, read and circle.

1 It's...

a a box. b an eraser. c a computer.

2 It's a...

a desk. b board. c backpack.

3 It's a...

a classroom. b bathroom. c backpack.

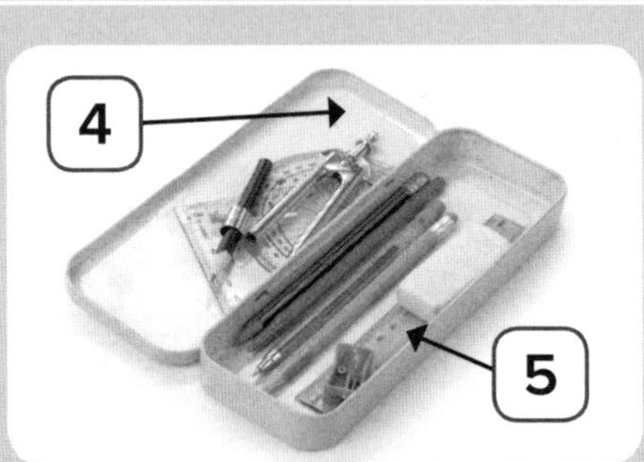

4 It's a...

a box. b backpack. c board.

5 The ruler is ... the box.

a in b next to c on

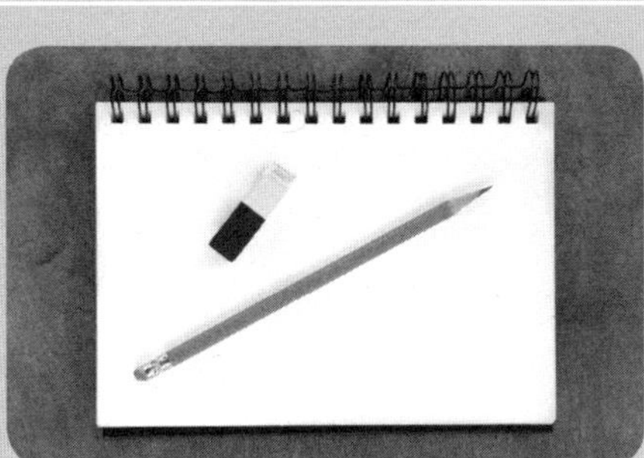

6 ... the pencil and eraser?

a Where are b Where's c Where

7 ... on the book.

a It's b They're c They

8 The books ... next to the backpack.

a is b are c they

2 Read again and check your answers.

1 Read, look and match.

1

3

☐ He's tall and funny.

She's tall and nice.

☐ They're loud and funny.

He's calm and nice.

☐ She's calm and strong.

☐ He's loud and short.

2

4

✧ **Listen and check.** 🔊 14

2 Mark (✓) the photos with friends.

☐ 

☐ 

☐ 

☐ 

Describing People

calm
funny
loud
nice
short
strong
tall

People

friend

How old are you?

What's your name?	My name's Gus.
How old are you?	I'm six.
Are you funny?	Yes, I am. / No, I'm not.

1 Read and match.

1 What's your name? 2 How old are you? 3 Are you strong?

a I'm six. b Yes, I am. c My name's Karl.

✧ **Listen and check.** 🔊15

2 Read and complete about you.

1 What's your name? My name's ....

2 How old are you? I'm ....

3 Are you strong? ....

1 Look, read and mark (✓ or ✗).

1 He's strong.

2 She's tall. He's short.

3 She's loud.

4 She's calm.

5 They're funny.

6 He's nice.

2 Trace the questions.

1 What's your name?

4 .... name's Carlos.

2 How old are you?

5 .... seven.

3 Are you tall?

6 No, I'm ....

✧ Complete the answers.

I'm My not

✧ Listen and check. 16

1 Match and make questions.

1 What's... — you calm?
2 How old... — your name?
3 Are... — are you?

4 What's your... — calm?
5 How old are... — you?
6 Are you... — name?

a **My** / **Your** name's Lidia.
b **I'm** / **You're** seven.
c Yes, **I'm not** / **I am**.

d My **name's** / **name** Nathan.
e **I** / **I'm** eight.
f No, **I am** / **I'm not**.

✧ **Circle the correct answers.**

2 Unscramble the questions.

1 your / What's / name

....?

2 are / old / How / you

....?

3 funny / you / Are

....?

a I'm **Trudy** / **Beth** / **Fiona**.
b I'm **seven** / **six** / **five**.
c Yes, I am!
And I'm **tall** / **short** / **strong**.

✧ **Listen and circle the answers.** 17

1 Read, look and match.

1 Four of my friends are tall. Three friends are short.

2 One friend is funny. Three friends are nice. Two friends are strong.

3 Six friends are loud! One friend is nice and calm.

2 Complete the interviews.

are I'm My Yes you your

1	2	3
What's .... name?	What's your name?	What's your name?
My name's Jane.	.... name's Lola.	My name's May.
How old are ....?	How old are you?	How old .... you?
I'm six.	.... five.	I'm seven.
Are you loud?	Are you strong?	Are you funny?
No, I'm not. I'm calm.	Yes, I am.	.........., I am.

✧ Read the interviews and label the children.

1 Look and unscramble.

1
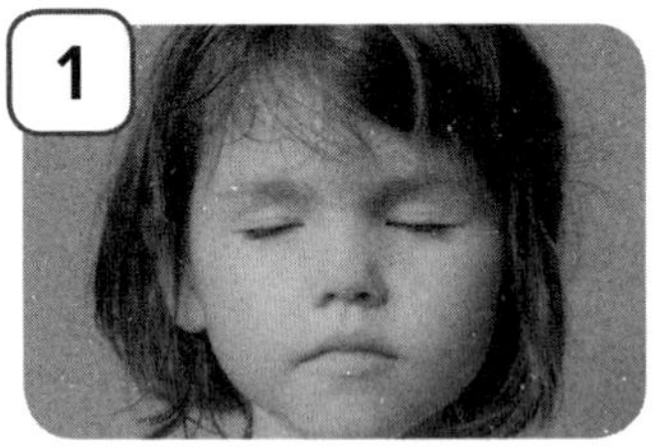
m a l

c ....

2

u n y n

f ....

3

d u o

l ....

4

c i e

n ....

5

r o h

s .... t

6

n o r

st .... g

7

l a l

t ....

8

e r i

f .... nd

✧ Find and circle the words.

a s t r o n g o u d
t e c a l m f o n y
r o l m e r t a l l
o n i s h o r t n d
k r u l f u n n y m
r d e n h s o c c i
s n i c e b e w d e
m a l c a l f e n d
f r i e n d r o n g
o r t a n l l o u d

1 Look, read and circle.

1 They're...

a calm. b nice. c loud.

2 "Is your friend tall?" "No, he's not. He's..."

a short. b strong. c loud.

3 "Is he ...?" "Yes, he is!"

a strong b loud c funny

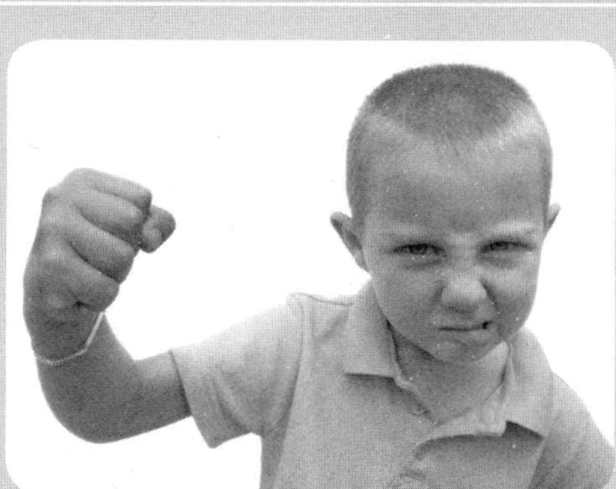

4 "Are you ...?" "No, I'm not!"

a nice b short c strong

5 "Are you strong?" "Yes, ..."

a I'm not. b I am. c I'm.

6 "... your name?"

a How b Are c What's

7 "... name's Esme."

a I b My c I'm

8 "... are you?" "I'm seven."

a What b How c How old

2 Read again and check your answers.

Topic 3 What's for lunch?

Fruits

apple
banana
grape
orange

Vegetables

carrot
onion
potato
tomato

1 Listen and number in order. 18

an apple

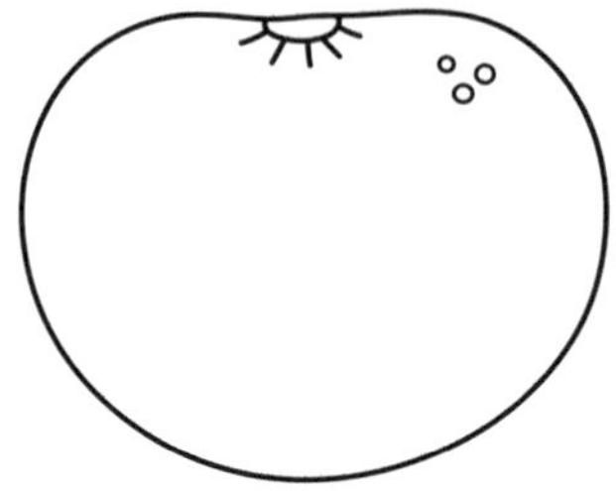

an orange

an onion

a carrot

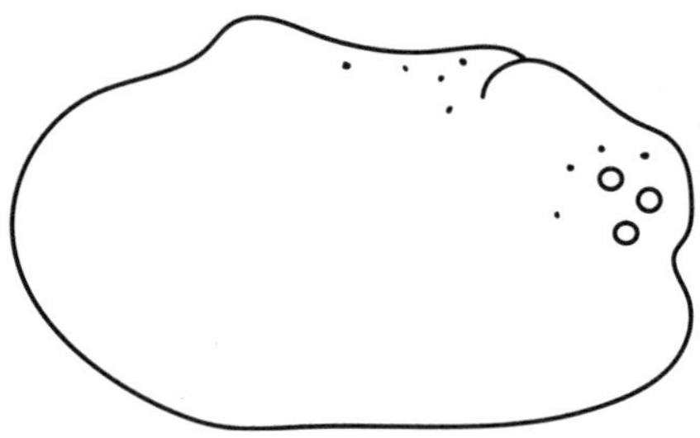

a potato

a tomato

a banana

a grape

Listen again and color.

There are some carrots.

There's an orange.
There are some carrots.
There aren't any grapes.

Are there any bananas?
Yes, there are. / No, there aren't.
How many carrots **are there?** Seven.

1 Listen and match. 19

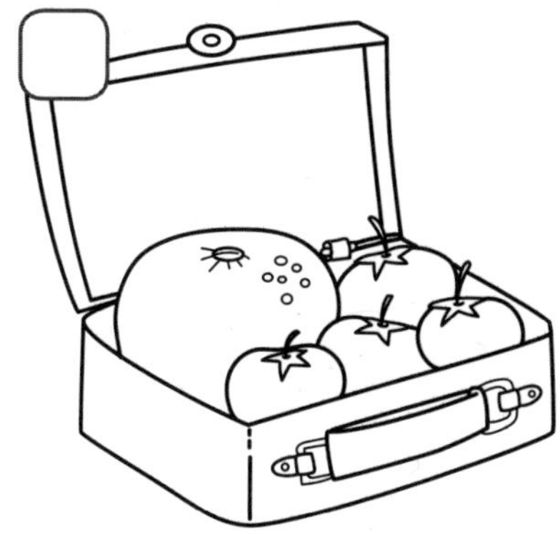

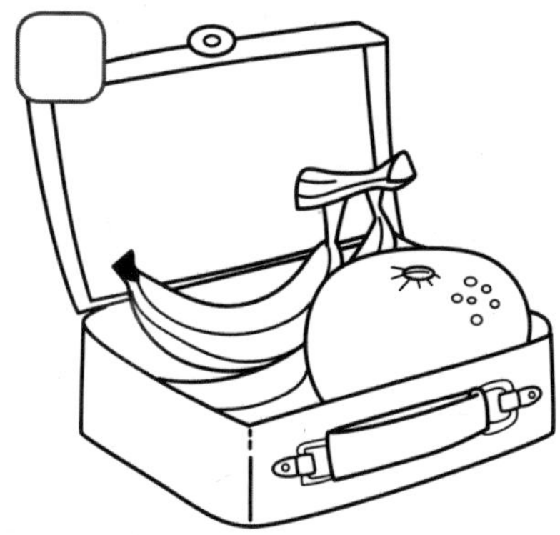

Listen again, look and circle.

1 **Is there / Are there** an orange in your lunch box? Yes, there **is / are**.

2 **There's / There are** an apple and there are two carrots.

3 Are there **any / some** bananas in your lunch box?

Yes, there are. There **is / are** two.

4 There are **any / some** grapes. And there's **a / an** apple.

1 Trace.

1 There's a tomato.

2 There are some potatoes.

3 There's a potato.

4 There are some tomatoes.

✧ Read, look and match.

2 Read and color the correct number of fruits and vegetables.

There are a lot of grapes.
There are eight.
There are three carrots.
There aren't any bananas.
There are two apples.
They're red.
There isn't an orange.
There are four onions.
They're purple.

1 Look, read and complete.

a	an	any	some

1 There's ………………………… onion.

2 There aren't ………………………… potatoes.

3 There are ………………………… apples.

4 There isn't ………………………… carrot.

✧ Look again. Read and match.

1 Is there a banana? a No, there aren't.

2 Is there an orange? b Yes, there is.

3 Are there any grapes? c No, there isn't.

4 Are there any tomatoes? d Yes, there are.

2 Listen and mark the fruits (✓ or ✗). 20

☐ 

☐ 

☐ 

☐ 

1 Trace and match.

1 carrots

2 onion

3 potato

4 tomatoes

5 peppers

6 cucumber

Vegetables

cucumber
pepper

2 Listen and complete. 21

1 How many tomatoes are there?

There are ....

2 Is there an onion?

....................................., there ....

3 Are there any potatoes?

Yes, there are. There are ....

4 Are there any peppers?

....................................., there .... Ew!

5 Are there any carrots?

Yes. There's .... carrot.

6 Is there an apple in the soup?

....................................., there .... It's vegetable soup!

1 Write the fruits and vegetables.

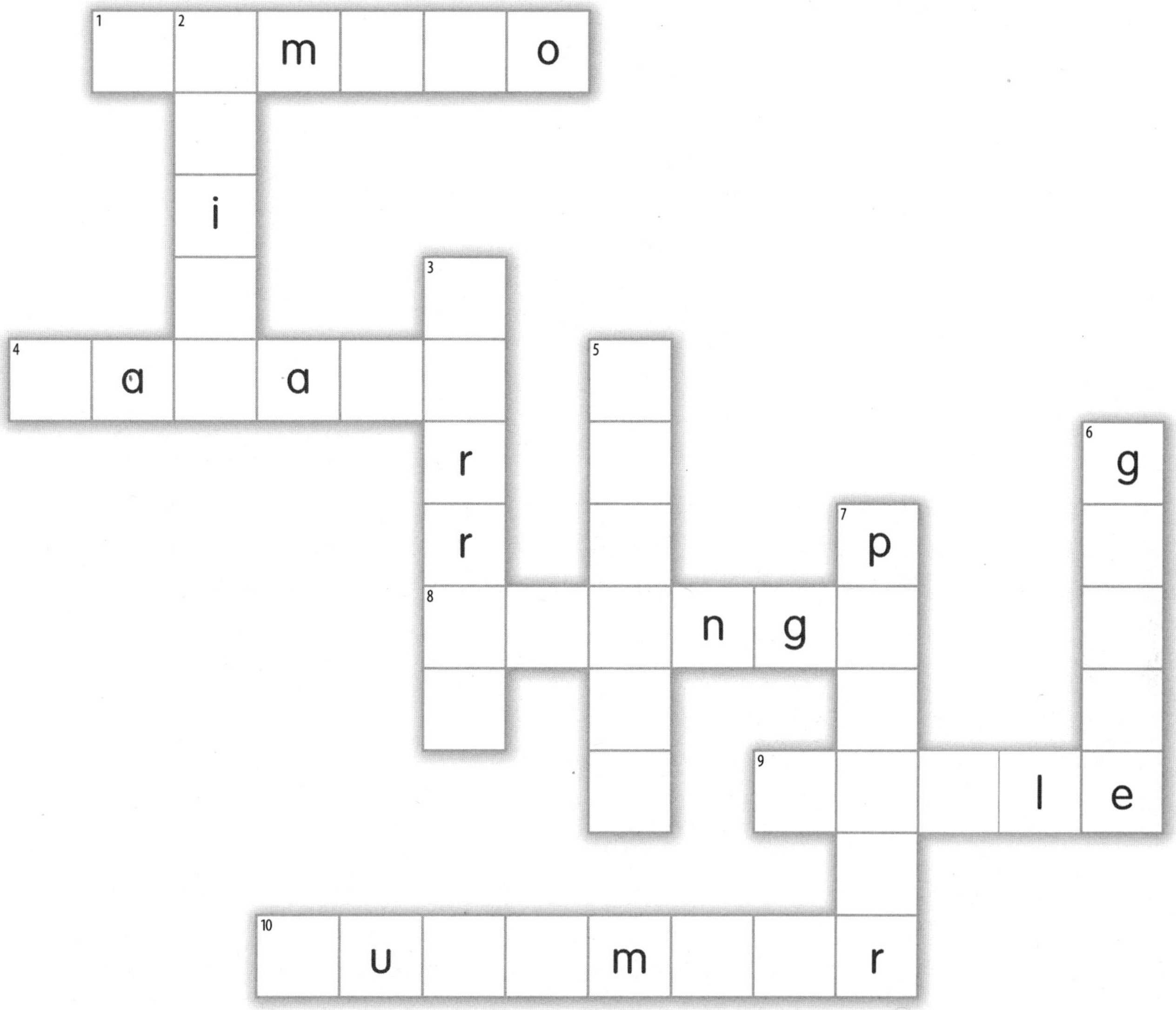

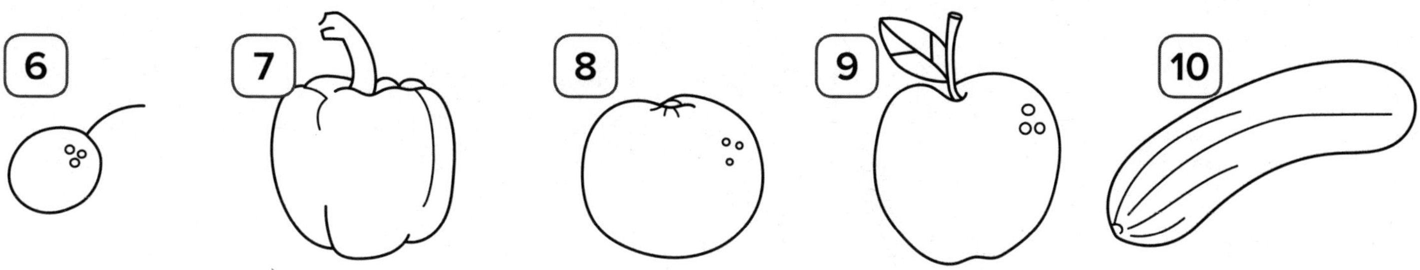

1 Look, read and circle.

1 There are three...

a peppers. b potatoes. c onions.

2 There's...

a an apple. b a carrot. c an orange.

3 There are some...

a bananas and apples.

b onions and tomatoes.

c cucumbers and peppers.

4 There aren't any...

a oranges. b apples. c grapes.

5 There ... a banana.

a isn't b aren't c is

6 There are ... grapes.

a a b any c some

7 "... potatoes are there?" "There are two."

a What b How many c Where

8 "... an onion?" "Yes, there is."

a Is there b There is c There are

2 Read again and check your answers.

1 Label the drinks and foods.

Drinks

1

2

3

Foods

4
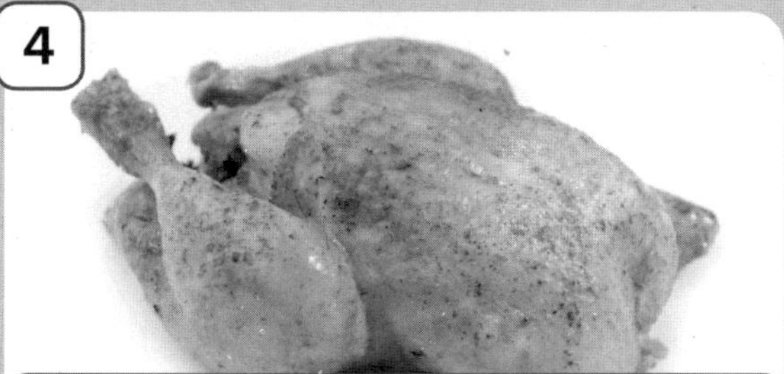

5

6
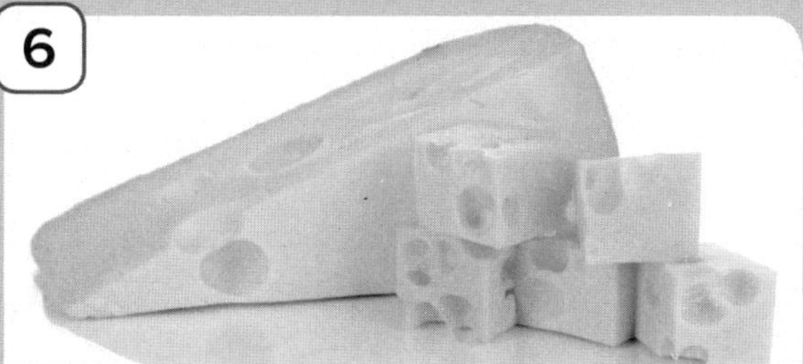

7

8

Drinks

juice
milk
water

Foods

bread
cheese
chicken
ice cream
lettuce

Listen and check. 22

There's some milk.

How much milk **is there?**
There isn't any milk.
There's some milk.
There's a lot of milk.

1 Read and match.

1

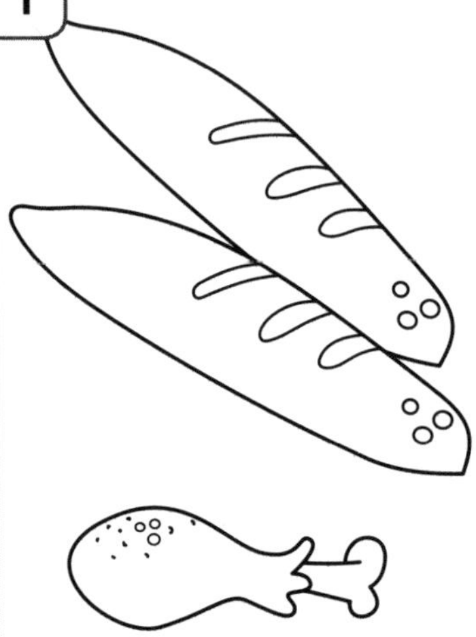

2

☐ Is there any water?
No, there isn't.
Is there any juice?
Yes, there is.

☐ How much chicken is there?
There's some.
How much bread is there?
There's a lot.

☐ Is there any ice cream?
Yes, there is.
How much ice cream is there?
There's a lot.

☐ How much milk is there?
There's a lot.
Is there any cheese?
Yes, there is.

3

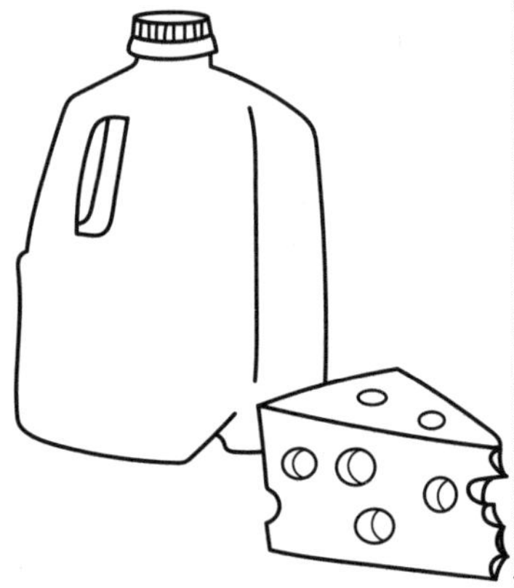

4

✧ **Listen and check.** 🔊23

1 Look, read and match.

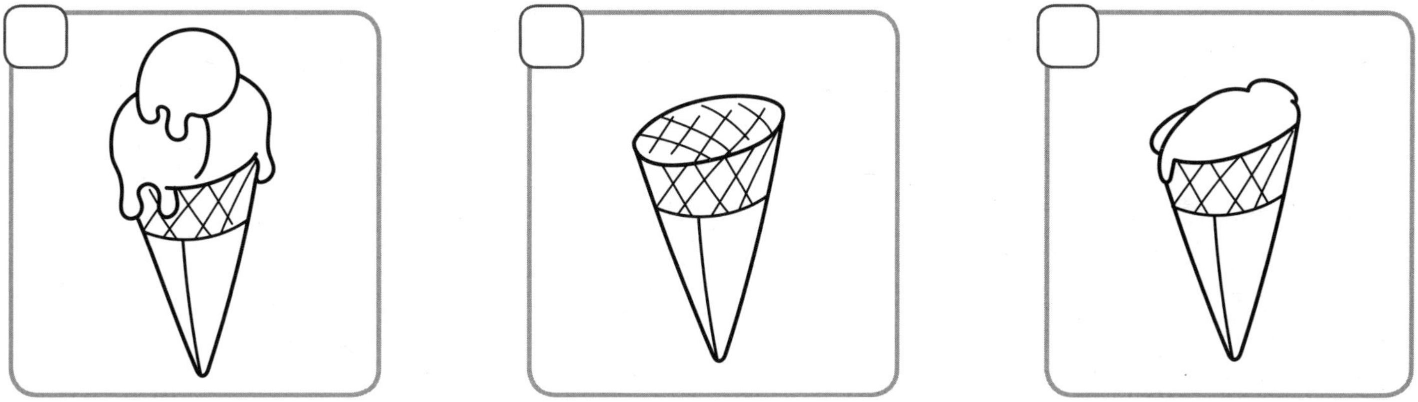

1 There isn't any ice cream.

2 There's some ice cream.

3 There's a lot of ice cream.

2 Listen and mark (✓) the correct picture. 24

1

2

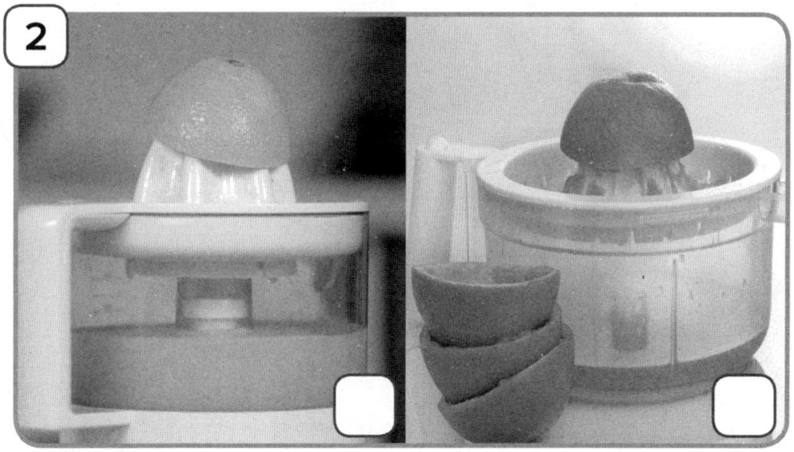

✧ Look and complete the conversations.

a lot	any	Is	isn't

1 **Girl:** Is there .... cheese?

Boy: Yes, there is.

Girl: How much cheese is there?

Boy: There's ....

2 **Girl:** .... there any juice?

Boy: Yes, there is.

Girl: Is there a lot?

Boy: No, there ....

✧ Listen again and check.

1 Look and mark (✓) the foods and drinks.

1 

bread	☐	lettuce	☐
cheese	☐	juice	☐
chicken	☐	milk	☐
ice cream	☐	water	☐

2 

bread	☐	lettuce	☐
cheese	☐	juice	☐
chicken	☐	milk	☐
ice cream	☐	water	☐

3 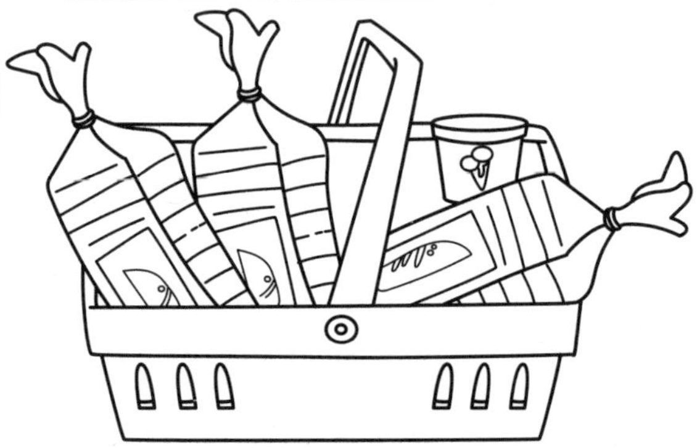

bread	☐	lettuce	☐
cheese	☐	juice	☐
chicken	☐	milk	☐
ice cream	☐	water	☐

Look at the pictures and complete.

a lot of   any   some

1 There's .... ice cream.

2 There's .... cheese. There's .... milk.

3 There isn't .... juice.

Look at the pictures and circle.

1 Is there any chicken? **Yes, there is. / No, there isn't.**

2 Is there any bread? **Yes, there is. / No, there isn't.**

3 How much ice cream is there? There's **a lot** / **some**.

1 Look and match.

1 They're sandwiches. 2 They're pizzas. 3 They're burgers.

2 Listen and match the names with the pizzas. 🔊25

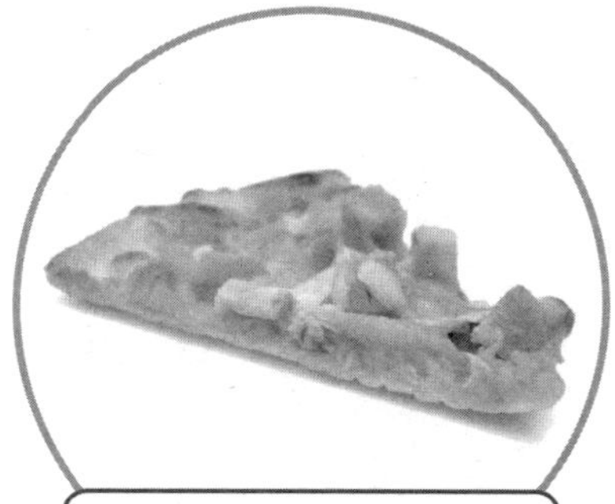

✦ **Circle the correct options. Then listen again and check.**

Foods

burger
pizza
sandwich

Carol: This pizza is delicious!

Gordon: Yeah. Is there **any** / **some** chicken on your pizza?

Carol: No, there **is** / **isn't**. It's cheese and tomato.

Gordon: Oh, I see! There's a lot of cheese.

Carol: Yes, there is. Is there any **burgers** / **chicken** on your pizza?

Gordon: Yes, there is.

Carol: **How much** / **What** chicken is there?

Gordon: Um, there's some chicken, not a lot. See?

1 Circle five differences in picture B.

A

B

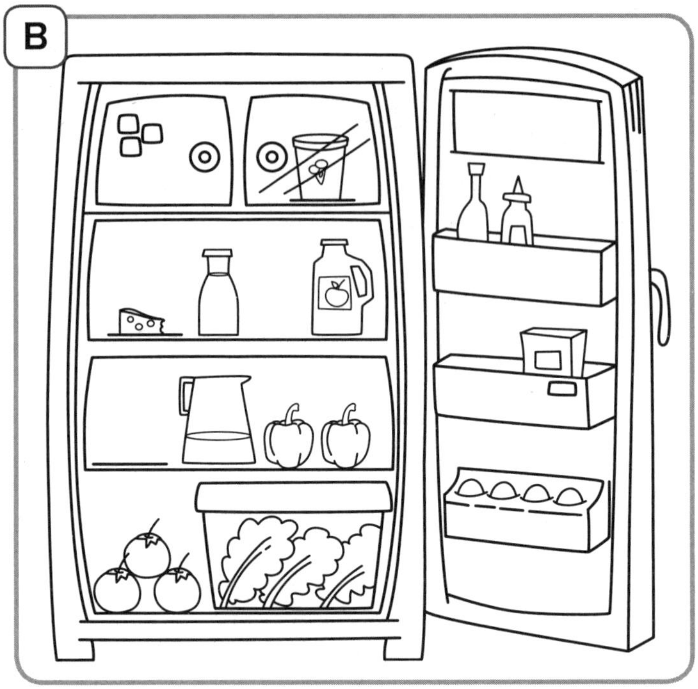

✧ **Read and write *A* or *B*.**

1 There's a lot of cheese. ☐

2 There's a lot of milk. ☐

3 There isn't any juice. ☐

4 There's some chicken. ☐

5 There's a lot of water. ☐

6 There's some cheese. ☐

7 There's some milk. ☐

8 There isn't any chicken. ☐

2 Unscramble and label.

....

2

3

1

....

....

1 Look, read and circle.

1 There's some...

a juice. b milk. c water.

2 There isn't any...

a ice cream. b bread. c cheese.

3 It's a...

a burger. b pizza. c sandwich.

4 There isn't any...

a lettuce. b cheese. c chicken.

5 Is there any cheese?

a Yes, there is.

b No, there isn't.

c There isn't any.

6 "How ... lettuce is there?" "There's some."

a lot

b many

c much

7 Is there ... water?

a lot b any c how

8 Yes, there is. There's...

a some. b a lot. c any.

2 Read again and check your answers.

Topic 4 What do I like?

Toys
ball
bike
car
doll

Pets
cat
dog
fish (pl. fish)
snake

1 Label the toys and pets.

Toys!

1 ....

2 ....

3 ....

4 ....

Pets!

5 ....

6 ....

7 ....

8 ....

✧ Listen and check. 26

2 Do you like these toys and pets? Circle ☺ or ☹.

Do you like fish?

I **like** snakes.
We **don't like** cats.
Do you **like** dogs?
Yes, I **do.** / No, I **don't.**

1 Look, read and circle.

1 Do you like dogs?

Yes, I do. / No, I don't.

2 Do you like cats?

Yes, I do. / No, I don't.

3

I **like** / **don't like** fish.

4

We **like** / **don't like** snakes.

✧ **Listen and check.** 27

2 Look and complete.

balls
bikes

1

I like ....

2

I don't like ....

1 Look, read and match.

1 I like dogs.

2 I don't like cats.

3 We like cats and dogs.

4 I don't like dogs.

2 Look, read and circle.

1

Do they like **bikes** / **dolls** / **cars**?

Yes, they do. / **No, they don't.**

2

Do they like **balls** / **bikes** / **cars**?

Yes, they do. / **No, they don't.**

✧ Answer about you.

1 Do you like dogs? ....

2 Do you like cats? ....

1 Look and circle.

1

We **don't like / like** ....

2

We **don't like / like** ....

3

We **don't like / like** ....

4

We **don't like / like** ....

Listen and write. 28

balls	bikes	cars	dolls

2 Match the questions, pictures and answers.

1 Do you like snakes?

2 Do you like fish?

3 Do you like cats?

Yes, I do.

No, I don't.

Yes, we do.

1 Listen. Match the children with the toys. 29

1

Sara

2

Luke

3

Wendy

4

Tom

2 Unscramble and match.

1 Do you like my ....?
Yes, I do!
s h i f

2 Do you like my ....?
Yes, I do!
l a b l

3 Do you like my ....?
Yes, I do!
o l d l

1 Look and read. Match the children with their rooms.

1

I like snakes. I don't like dolls.
I like cars. I don't like bikes or balls.

2

I don't like fish. I like cats.
I like cars, but I don't like balls.

3

I like dogs and fish.
I don't like bikes, but I like dolls.

4

I like dolls and cars.
I don't like cats. I like snakes.

1 Look, read and circle.

1 a "I like dolls."

b "You like bikes."

c "Do you like cars?"

2 a "Yes, we do."

b "We like bikes."

c "No, we don't."

3 "Do you like ...?"

a dogs b cats c fish

4 a "Yes, I do."

b "No, they don't."

c "Yes, we do."

5 "Do you like ...?"

a dolls b bikes c balls

6 a "You like bikes."

b "No, we don't."

c "Yes, we do."

7 "Do you like ...?"

a fish b dogs c snakes

8 a "No, I'm not."

b "No, I don't."

c "No, we aren't."

2 Read again and check your answers.

1 Label the pictures.

1

.... ☺ ☹

2

.... ☺ ☹

3

.... ☺ ☹

4

.... ☺ ☹

5

.... ☺ ☹

6

.... ☺ ☹

7

.... ☺ ☹

8

.... ☺ ☹

Activities

dancing
drawing
painting
reading
singing

Entertainment

computer games
movies
sports

✧ **Listen and check.** 🔊30

2 Do you like them, too? Circle ☺ or ☹.

He likes reading.

He likes reading.
She doesn't like painting.
Does she like sports?
Yes, she does. / No, she doesn't.

1 Look, read and match.

1 He likes singing.

2 He likes dancing.

3 She doesn't like reading.

4 She doesn't like painting.

2 Look and complete.

Do do Does doesn't

1

.... they like dancing?

Yes, they ....

2

.... he like movies?

No, he ....

✦ **Listen and check.** 31

1 Label the activities.

computer games   dancing   drawing   reading   singing   sports

1 ....

2 ....

3 ....

4 ....

5 ....

6 ....

✧ What does Ruby like? Listen and mark the activities (✓ or ✗). 32

✧ Draw Ruby's present.

1 Read and label the children.

1 Tom likes sports.
2 Jon and Lisa like dancing.
3 Ana doesn't like painting.
4 Alan doesn't like drawing.
5 Lily likes computer games.
6 Beth and Ben don't like reading.

✧ Read and match.

1 Does Alan like drawing?
2 Do Beth and Ben like reading?
3 Does Tom like sports?
4 Do Jon and Lisa like dancing?
5 Does Ana like painting?
6 Does Lily like computer games?

a Yes, they do.
b No, she doesn't.
c Yes, he does.
d Yes, she does.
e No, they don't.
f No, he doesn't.

✧ Listen and check. 33

1 Look and complete.

1

He likes ....

2

They like ....

3

They ....

4

She ....

2 Look. Complete the questions. Circle the answers.

1

Do they like ....?

Yes, they do. / No, they don't.

2

Do they like ....?

Yes, they do. / No, they don't.

3

Does he like ....?

Yes, he does. / No, he doesn't.

4

Does she like ....?

Yes, she does. / No, she doesn't.

1 Find eight entertainment words and activities.

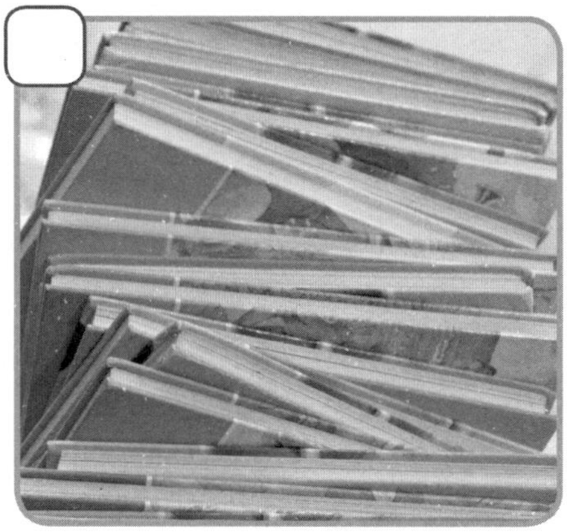

[1] c	o	m	p	u	t	e	r	g	a	m	e	s
n	[2] d	e	r	d	i	n	g	f	d	s	l	k
d	r	n	g	d	a	d	[3] s	p	o	r	t	[4] s
e	a	[5] d	a	n	c	i	n	g	o	o	l	i
c	w	h	o	i	h	o	w	i	n	g	[6] m	n
e	i	h	[7] p	a	i	n	t	i	n	g	o	g
t	n	h	i	n	g	h	k	w	q	m	v	i
i	g	m	o	v	e	s	p	i	r	t	i	n
n	i	n	g	l	y	r	e	a	d	i	e	g
g	s	[8] r	e	a	d	i	n	g	e	t	s	e

✧ **Number the pictures.**

1 Look, read and circle.

1 She likes...

a singing b reading. c dancing.

2 He likes...

a painting. b singing. c drawing.

3 They like...

a computer games. b movies. c sports.

4 They like...

a painting. b drawing. c reading.

5 "Do ... like singing?"

a he b she c they

6 a "Yes, they do."

b "Yes, they are."

c "No, they don't."

7 "... like sports?"

a Does she b Do they c Does he

8 a "Yes, he does."

b "Yes, she does."

c "Yes, they do."

2 Read again and check your answers.

Topic 5 Who are my friends and family?

1 Label the family members.

Family Members

brother
father/dad
grandfather
grandmother
mother/mom
sister

1

2

3

✧ Listen and check. 34

2 Look, read and match.

1 My family has a mom, a dad, three sisters and me. I'm the boy!

2 In my family, there's my grandmother and grandfather, my mom, my sister and me. I'm the small girl!

3 This is my family and me. I have a grandfather, a mother and a father, and a brother. I'm the girl!

✧ Circle "me" in each family.

Do you have any brothers and sisters?

I have two sisters.
We don't have any brothers.
Do you have any brothers and sisters?
Yes, I do. / No, I don't.
How many sisters **do you have?** Two.

1 Look, read and match.

1

2

3

4

5

6

a I don't have any brothers and sisters.
b I have two brothers. I don't have any sisters.
c I have two sisters.
d I have one brother.
e I have one sister.
f I have three brothers. I don't have a sister.

✦ **Listen and check.** 🔊35

2 Unscramble and answer the question.

Do you / brothers and sisters / have any

....?

....

1 Look, read and match.

1 How many brothers do you have, Paul?
2 Lisa, how many brothers do you have?
3 How many sisters do you have, Gaby?
4 Dan, how many sisters do you have?
5 How many brothers do you have, Jen?

a I don't have any brothers.
b I have two brothers.
c I have four sisters.
d I have one brother.
e I have one sister.

Listen and check. 36

2 Read and draw the family.

My name's Camilla. I'm seven. I have one sister, Poppy. Poppy's three years old. I have two brothers, Felix and Dan. Felix is ten and Dan is twelve. They like sports. I also have a mom, a dad and a grandmother. There are seven people in my family!

1 Read, look and match.

1

I have a mom, a dad and one sister. I don't have any brothers.

2

I have a mom and I have a grandmother. I have two sisters.

3

I don't have any brothers and sisters. I have a dad and a grandmother!

4

I have a dad, a grandfather and one brother. I don't have a grandmother or a mother.

2 Look, read and complete.

have   don't have

These are my toys. I (1)..............................

a ball. I (2).............................. a toy car.

I (3).............................. a lot of dolls, only one!

I (4).............................. a bike.

1 Read and write.

don't have   don't like   have   I'm   like

Hi, I'm Carol. (1)................ seven. Let's be friends! I (2)................ any brothers and sisters. I (3)................ one pet: my cat, Suzy. I don't have a dog. I (4)................ dogs! I (5)................ sports. I have two balls and a bike. How about you?

✧ Match.

1 Do you have any brothers and sisters?
2 Do you have any pets?
3 Do you like toys?

a Yes, I do. I have a cat.
b No, I don't.
c Yes, I do. Especially my bike!

✧ Listen and mark (✓). Then circle a friend for Carol. 37

Name	Family	Pets	Likes
1 	☐ brothers ☐ sisters	☐ cat ☐ dog	☐ sports ☐ dancing
2 	☐ brothers ☐ sisters	☐ cat ☐ fish	☐ computer games ☐ movies
3 	☐ brothers ☐ sisters	☐ snake ☐ cat	☐ sports ☐ reading

1 Look and write the family members.

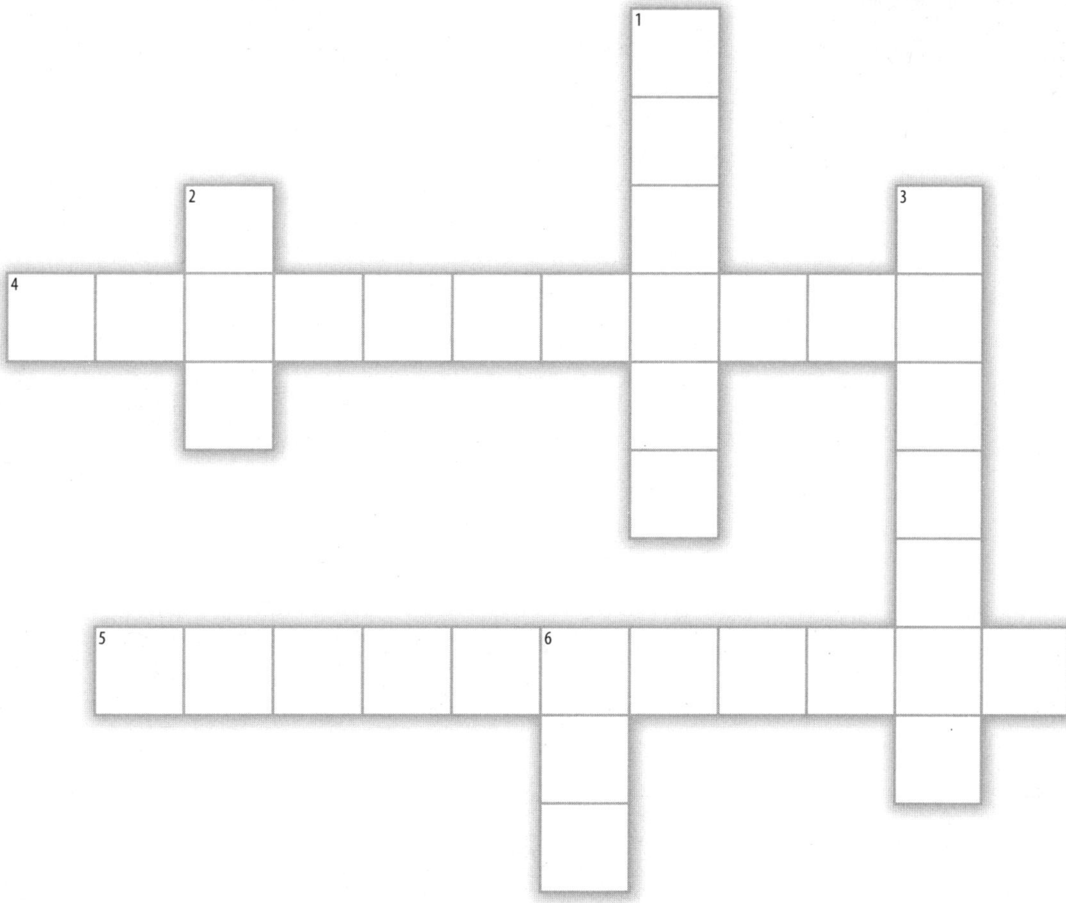

2 Unscramble the words and label the photo.

berthor

hafter

rothem

tisser

1 Look, read and circle.

1 "She's my..."

a sister. b mom. c grandmother.

2 "She's my..."

a sister. b mother. c brother.

3 "He's my..."

a dad. b brother. c grandfather.

4 "He's my..."

a dad. b brother. c grandfather.

5 "I ... one brother and one sister."

a am b have c don't have

6 "... any brothers and sisters?"

a Do you have

b Do you

c Have you

7 a "No, I don't."

b "No, I'm not."

c "Not."

8 "... pets do you have?" "Two!"

a Where

b What

c How many

2 Read again and check your answers.

1 Look at the hair. Circle three adjectives for each child.

1

curly / straight

short / long

brown / blond

2

curly / straight

short / long

brown / black

3

curly / straight

short / long

brown / black

4

curly / straight

short / long

black / blond

Parts of the Body

eye
hair

Colors

black
blond
brown

Hair Types

curly
long
straight

✧ **Listen and check.** 38

2 Look and complete.

eyes
hair

I have brown ....

I have short ....

He has long hair.

He has long hair.
They have curly hair.
She doesn't have green eyes.
Does she have brown eyes?
Yes, she does. / No, she doesn't.

1 Read and match.

1 

2 

3 

4 

☐ She has blond hair and brown eyes.

☐ He has brown hair and brown eyes. His hair is short.

☐ He has black hair. It's curly.

☐ They have blond hair. It's not curly.

✦ Look, read and circle.

1 Does he have short hair? **Yes, he does. / No, he doesn't.**

2 Does he have long hair? **Yes, he does. / No, he doesn't.**

3 Does she have curly hair? **Yes, she does. / No, she doesn't.**

4 Do they have curly hair? **Yes, they do. / No, they don't.**

✦ Listen and check. 39

1 Read and mark (✓ or ✗).

1 "We have black hair." ☐

2 "My dad has long hair." ☐

3 "I have one sister. We have long hair." ☐

4 "My mom has curly hair." ☐

2 Look and complete.

doesn't   don't   has   have

1

They don't have long hair.

They .... short hair.

2

She doesn't have straight hair.

She .... curly hair.

3

They ....

.... black hair. They have blond hair.

4

She .... short hair. She .... long hair.

1 Read and draw.

1

My mom has long hair. It's straight.

2

My dad has short hair. It's curly.

3

My grandmother has long hair. It's straight.

4

My brother has long hair. It's curly.

✧ **Listen and color.** 🔊40

2 Unscramble the questions. Look and circle the answers.

1

he / have / Does / blond hair

....?

Yes, he does. / No, he doesn't.

2

have / they / straight hair / Do

....?

Yes, they do. / No, they don't.

3

Does / long hair / have / she

....?

Yes, she does. / No, she doesn't.

1 Read, look and match.

1 They're sisters. They have brown hair. It's long and straight. They like reading!

2 She's his big sister. They have blond hair. He has short hair. She has long hair. They like bikes!

3 They're friends. He has curly hair. It's short. She has straight hair. They like sports!

2 Listen. Match the children with their pets. 41

Ben Lynn Rose Tom

✧ Look, read and complete.

doesn't don't has

1 **Ben:** My cat .... short hair.

2 **Lynn:** My cat .... have any hair!

3 **Rose:** My dog .... long hair.

4 **Tom:** My dogs .... have long hair. They have short hair!

1 Trace a path to the barber. Follow the words for hair.

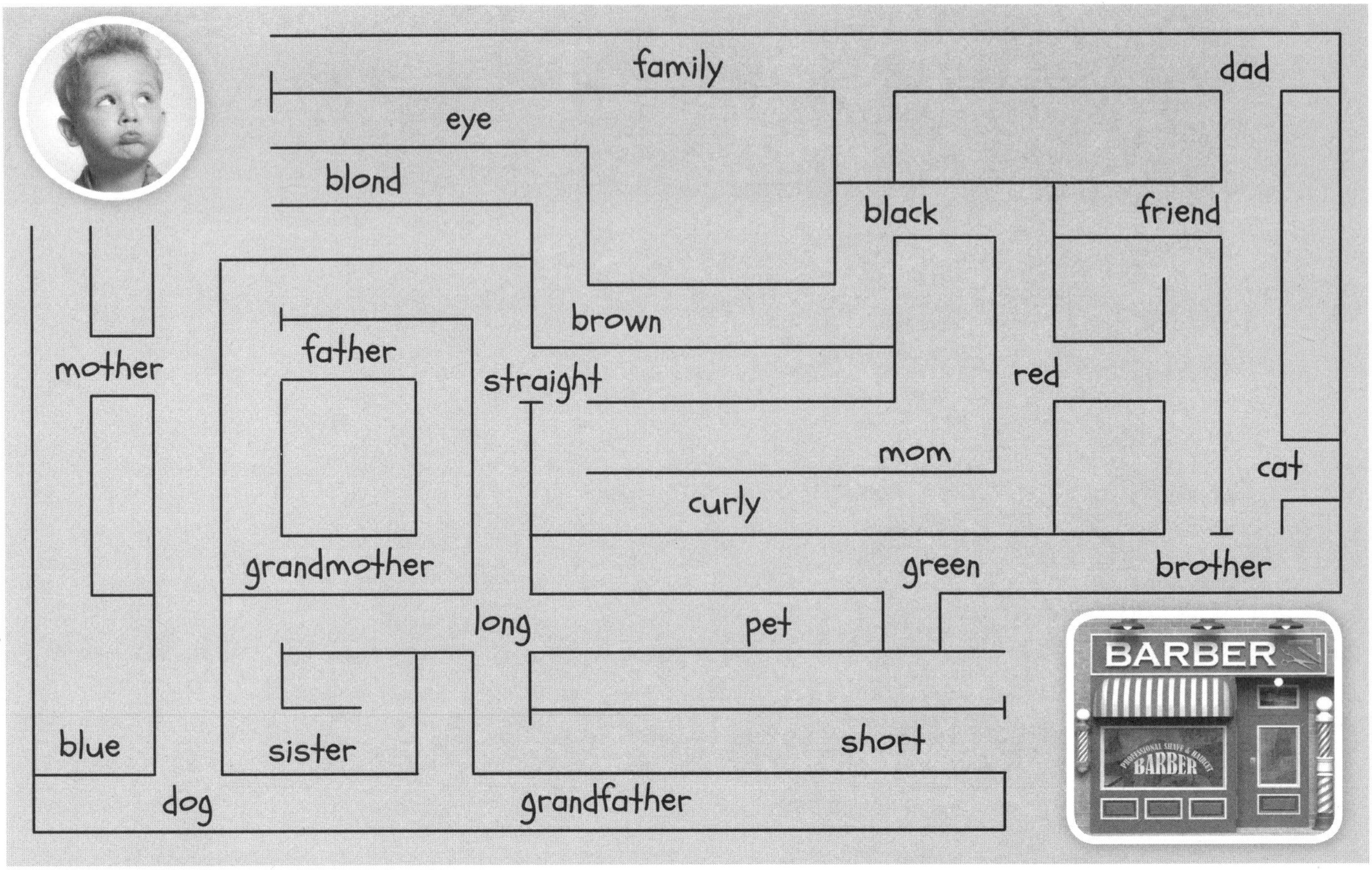

2 Unscramble.

1 My dog has .... (clabk) hair. It's .... (horst) and .... (cyrul).

2 My dog has .... (nobld) hair. It's .... (glon) and .... (ratghist).

3 My dog doesn't have any .... (irah)!

✧ Read and match.

☐ 

☐ 

☐ 

1 Look, read and circle.

1 My grandfather has ... hair.

a short b curly c long

2 His hair is...

a blue. b black. c blond.

3 "Does she have ... hair?"

"Yes, she does."

a short b curly c straight

4 Her dog has ... hair.

a blond b black c red

5 "Does she have green eyes?"

"No, she ...! She has blue eyes."

a don't b isn't c doesn't

6 "Her cat ... green eyes."

a doesn't b has c have

7 "... the mother have straight hair?"

"Yes, she does."

a Do b Does c Has

8 They ... have blond hair.

a don't b aren't c doesn't

2 Read again and check your answers.

Topic 6 What am I good at?

Sports
baseball
basketball
hockey
soccer
table tennis
tennis
volleyball

Actions
play

1 Label the sports.

WE PLAY SPORTS!

1

....

....

2

....

3

....

4

....

5

....

6

....

7

....

Listen and check. 42

2 Read and guess the sports.

1 You play in teams of five. The ball is orange. ....

2 There are two or four players. The ball is yellow. ....

3 You don't play this sport with a ball. ....

1 Look, read and match.

1

2

3

4

5
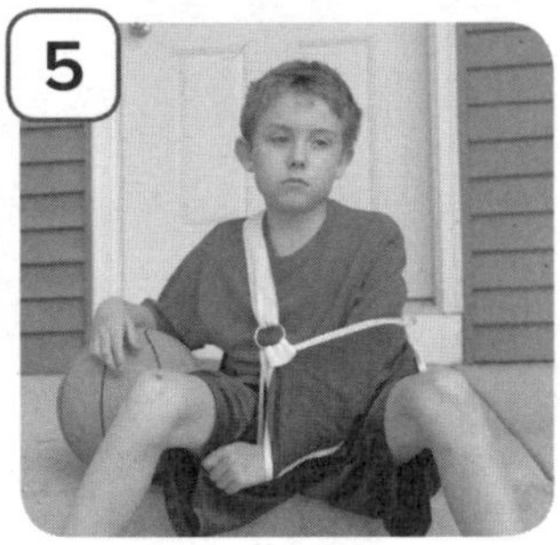

6

I can sing.

I can sing. **They can't** read.

- ☐ They can't play hockey.
- ☐ They can play basketball.
- ☐ He can't play baseball.
- ☐ They can play hockey.
- ☐ They can play baseball.
- ☐ He can't play basketball.

✧ **Listen and check.** 43

2 Look, read and complete.

can	can't

1 I .... play computer games.

2 My dad .... play computer games.

3 Circle for you.

1 I **can** / **can't** play computer games.

2 I **can** / **can't** play volleyball.

3 I **can** / **can't** sing.

4 I **can** / **can't** dance.

1 Look, read and match.

☐ My dad is good at music. He can play the guitar.

☐ My friend can't walk, but he's good at basketball.

1

2

3

4

5

6

☐ My friends can play soccer. They play on the school team.

☐ My sisters are good at drawing. They can draw very well.

✧ Complete about the other two photos.

5 My friend .... walk. But he .... play soccer.

6 My brother can't .... He's two years old!

✧ Listen and check. 44

1 Look and complete.

1

My grandmother and grandfather can play ....

2

I can play .... with my dad. He's strong!

3

My dad and sister can .... baseball. They're good!

4

My grandmother's bad at tennis. She .... tennis well.

5

My baby sister .... hockey. She's small.

6

He .... volleyball today. He doesn't have a ball!

✦ **Listen and check.** 45

1 Read, look and write the sports.

You can play some sports with a ball, like  (1)........................ and  (2)......................... You can play some sports with two or four people, like  (3)........................ and  (4)........................ .... You can play some sports on the beach, like  (5)........................ and  (6)......................... And you can play some sports on ice or grass, like  (7).........................

2 Read and match.

1 This sport has a big, orange ball.

2 You can play this sport on a table.

3 This sport has a yellow ball.

4 You can play this sport on ice or grass.

a table tennis

b hockey

c tennis

d basketball

3 Look and complete.

I can play

....

I can ....

....

I ....

....

....

1 Look and write the sports.

Across

1

4

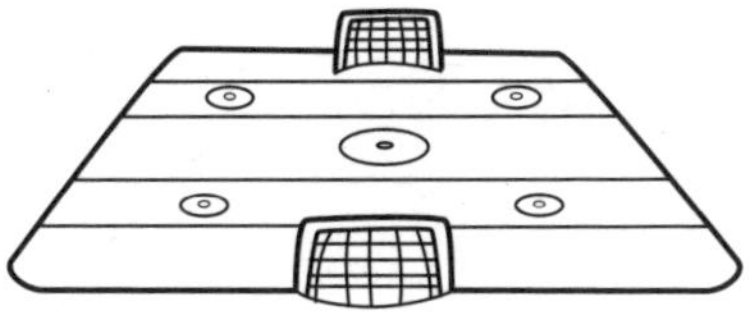

5

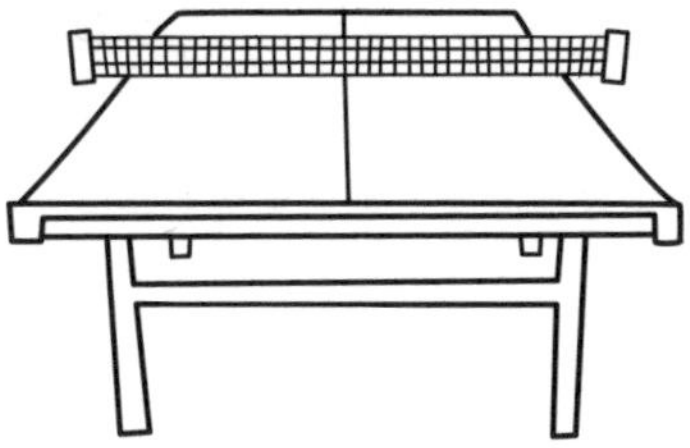

6

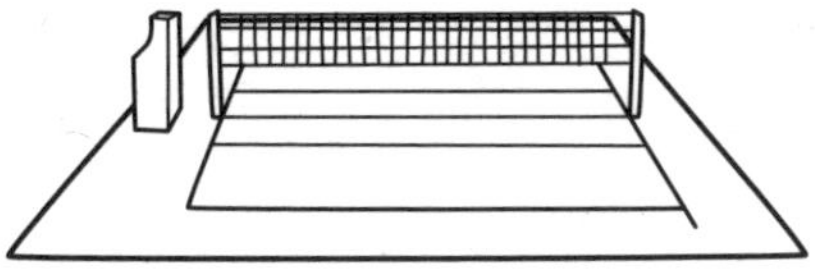

Down

1

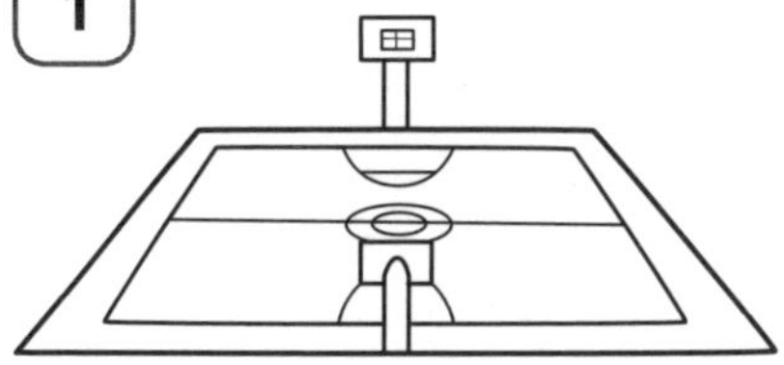

2

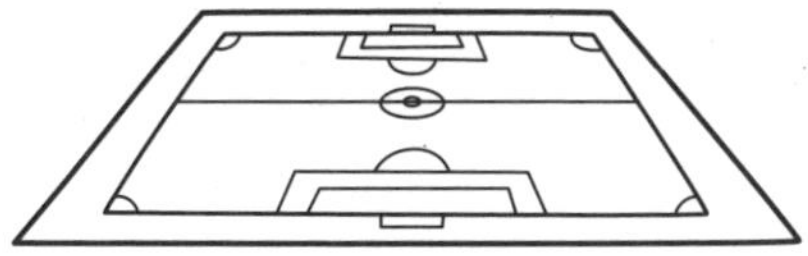

3

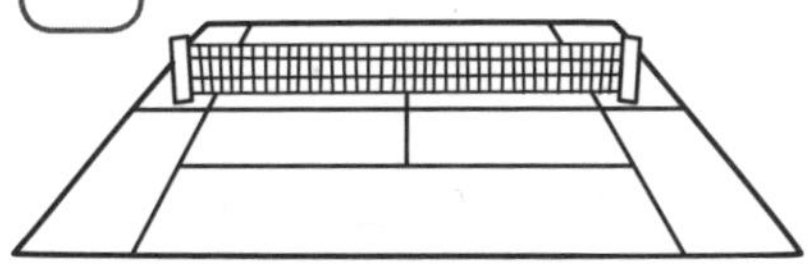

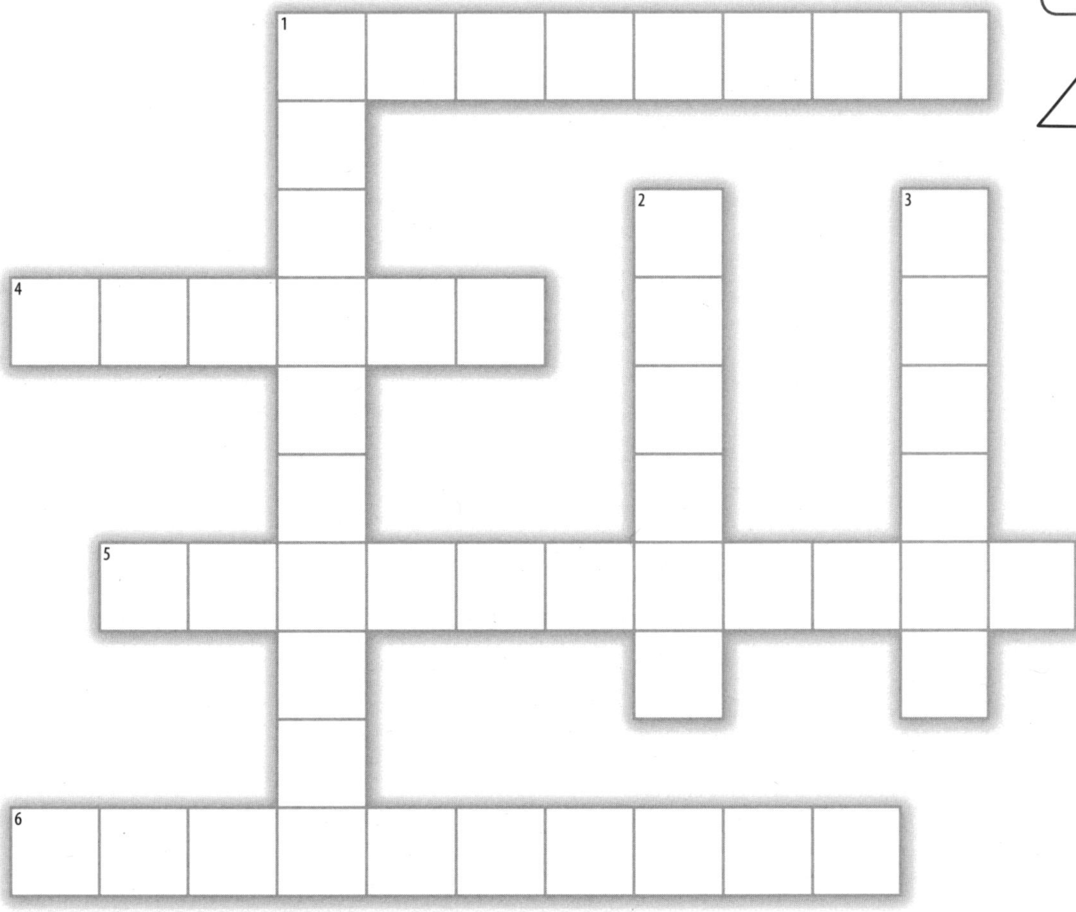

1 Look, read and circle.

1 This field is for...

a baseball. b basketball. c soccer.

2 We ... today. It's cold!

a can play b can't play c play

3 He likes...

a hockey. b table tennis. c tennis.

4 But he ... play today.

a can b does c can't

5 This sport is...

a hockey. b volleyball. c soccer.

6 They're small, but they ... play!

a can b can't c not

7 This ball is for...

a volleyball. b soccer. c baseball.

8 We ... play today.

a are b can't c can

2 Read again and check your answers.

1 Look, read and complete.

Actions
catch
hit
jump
kick
ride
run
swim
throw

1 

He can .... a bike.

2 

She can .... a ball.

3 

He can .... a ball.

4 

She can .... a ball.

5 

They can ....

6 

He can ....

7 

They can ....

8 

She can .... a ball.

✧ **Listen and check.** 46

2 Circle the actions.

Can you run?

Can you run?
Yes, I **can.** / **No,** I **can't.**
What can you do?
I **can** catch a ball.

1 Look, read and complete.

1

What sport can she ....?
She can play ....
Can she hit the ball?
................................, she can.

2

What sport .... he play?
He can .... baseball.
Can he catch the ball?
................................, he can't.

3

What sport can .... play?
They can play ....
.... they jump?
Yes, they can.

4

What sport .... play?
They can play soccer.
Can they kick the ball?
Yes, they ....

✧ **Listen and check.** 47

1 Look, read and circle.

1

They **can** / **can't** run, and they **can** / **can't** jump. But they **can** / **can't** play basketball! They can **throw** / **kick** and **hit** / **catch** the ball.

2

He can **ride** / **run** a bike. She **can** / **can't** ride a bike. She's three years old! But she **can** / **can't** run!

2 Unscramble the questions.

1

it / Can / swim

....?

Yes, it can. / No, it can't.

2

Can / catch / it

....?

Yes, it can. / No, it can't.

3

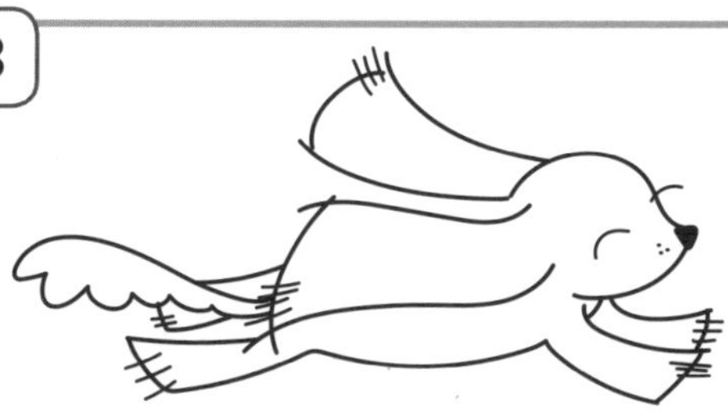

run / it / Can

....?

Yes, it can. / No, it can't.

4

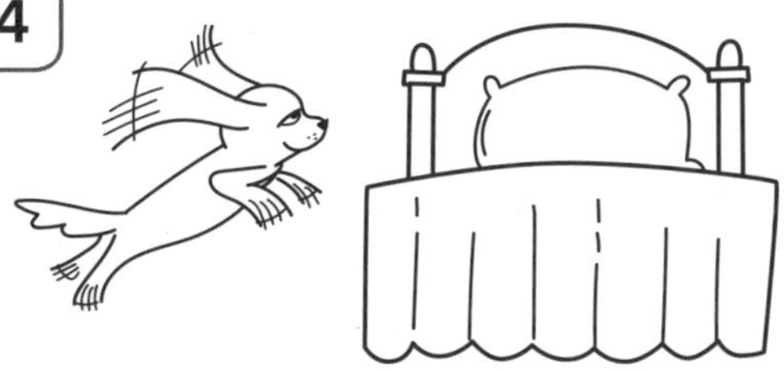

Can / jump / it

....?

Yes, it can. / No, it can't.

✧ **Look and circle the answers.**

1 Read and complete.

My name's Greta and this is my cat, Slinky.

I'm good at some sports. I **kick / play / throw** basketball at school. I'm tall and I can **kick / swim / jump**. And I'm good at soccer. I can **kick / catch / run** the ball.

But I don't like tennis or baseball. I can't **play / hit / jump** the ball.

Slinky can't **run / hit / swim**. She doesn't like water.

But she can run fast and she can **catch / hit / jump** mice!

Do you have any pets? What can they do?

Write soon! Bye!

2 What can the pets do? Listen and mark (✓ or ✗). 48

1

- ☐ catch a ball
- ☐ jump
- ☐ run

2

- ☐ ride a bike
- ☐ kick a ball
- ☐ catch a ball

✦ Complete about the pets with *can* or *can't*.

1 Lucky .... catch a ball and she .... run. She .... jump.

2 Beaker .... ride a bike. He .... kick a ball, too. But he .... catch a ball.

1 Listen and mark (✓ or ✗). 49

Name: Barney	Name: Jen	Name: Tara
☐ catch a ball	☐ swim	☐ run
☐ run	☐ jump	☐ catch a ball
☐ kick a ball	☐ throw a ball	☐ hit a ball
Sport:	Sport:	Sport: ....

✧ **Choose a sport for each student.**

baseball   basketball   soccer

2 Unscramble the questions and answer for you.

1 play / What / can / sports / you

....?

....

2 a ball / catch / Can / you

....?

....

3 a baseball / Can / hit / you

....?

....

1 Connect the words.

r	ide
k	un
c	atch
t	wim
s	hrow
r	ump
j	ick
h	it

✧ **Match the words with the pictures.**

2 Sort the sports actions.

1

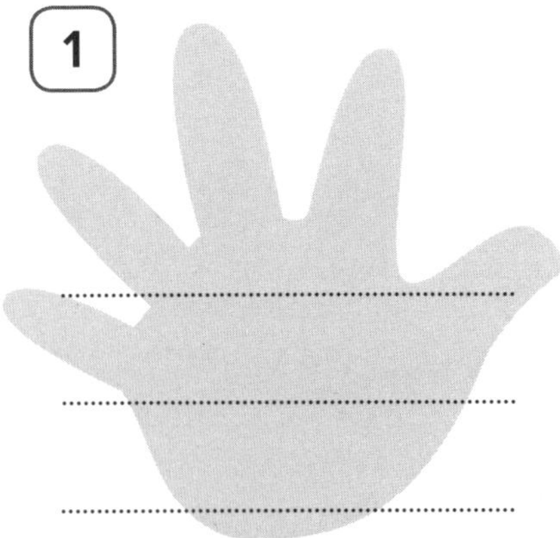

We do this with our hands.

2

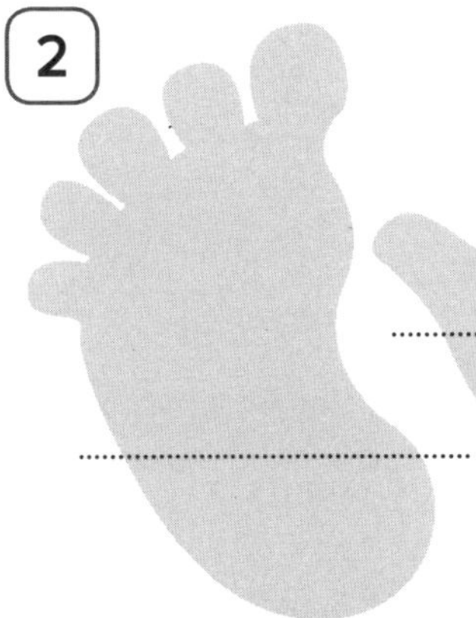

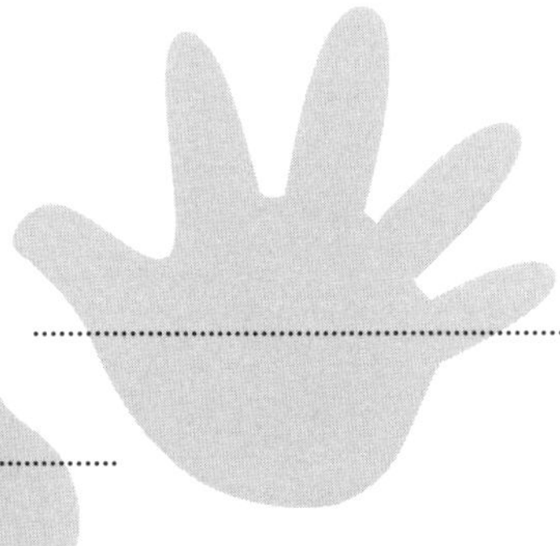

We do this with our hands and feet.

3

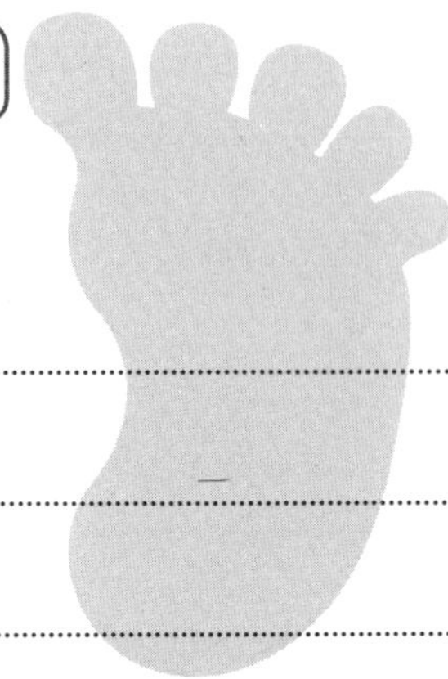

We do this with our feet.

1 Look, read and circle.

1 "Can you ... a bike?"

a run b throw c ride

2 "No, I..."

a can. b can't. c not.

3 "Can you play volleyball?"

"Yes, ..."

a you can. b I can. c we can.

4 "I can jump and ... a ball."

a kick b hit c run

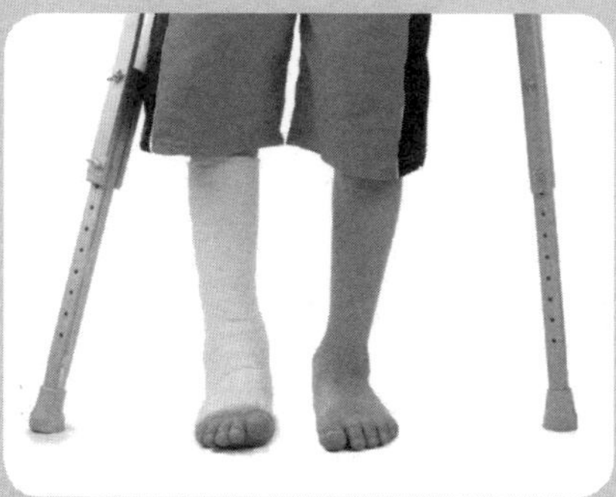

5 "What sports can you...?"

a hit b run c play

6 "I'm good at basketball. But I ... play today."

a can b can't c aren't

7 "... play tennis today?"

"No, I can't."

a Can b You can c Can you

8 "... can you do?"

"I can watch movies!"

a Where b How c What

2 Read again and check your answers.

Topic 7 What do children in other countries do?

Routines

go to bed
go to school
live
speak
wake up

Countries

China
Russia
Spain

Languages

Chinese
Russian
Spanish

1 Unscramble and label the countries

paniS saiRus niCha

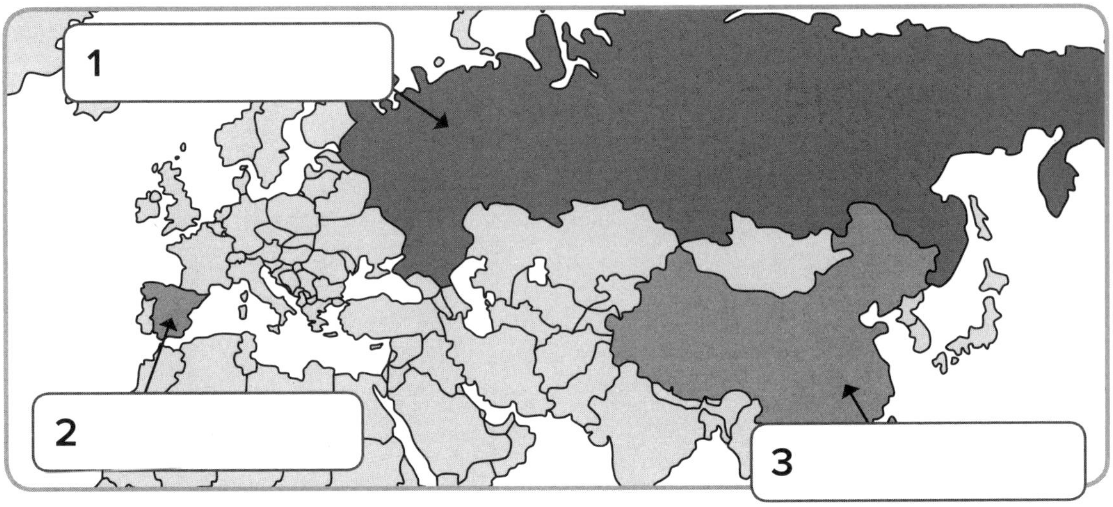

2 Write the routines.

....

go to ....

go to ....

✧ Listen and complete. 50

1 **Sunny:** I live in China. I .... Chinese and English.

I wake up at .... o'clock in the morning.

2 **Alba:** I live in Spain. I speak two languages: Spanish and English.

I .... to school at .... o'clock.

3 **Alexei:** I .... in Russia. I speak Russian and English.

I go to bed at .... o'clock.

He doesn't like fish.

He speaks English.

He lives in France.
He speaks English.
She likes cheese.
She doesn't like fish.

1 Look and match.

1 John lives in Canada. He speaks English and Inuktitut.

2 He wakes up at seven o'clock.

3 He goes to school at eight o'clock.

4 He goes to bed at seven o'clock.

2 Read and circle.

1

Shu **lives** / **speaks** in China. She **lives** / **speaks** two Chinese languages—Mandarin and Cantonese—and English, too. She **goes** / **has** a cat. She **doesn't like** / **doesn't go** dogs.

2

Javi **goes** / **lives** in Spain. He **lives** / **speaks** three languages: Spanish, Catalan and English. He **plays** / **has** soccer. He **doesn't have** / **doesn't like** baseball.

Listen and check. 51

1 Complete the words.

–a –ain –an –ese –ish

1 

2 

3 

1 Andriy lives in Russi.......... . He speaks Russi.......... and Engl.......... .

2 Chen lives in Chin.......... . She speaks Chin.......... and Engl.......... .

3 Lola lives in Sp.......... . She speaks Span.......... .

✧ **Write about you.**

I live in .... I speak ....

2 Label the actions.

go to bed go to school wake up

....

✧ **Number the actions in order.**

1 Look, read and circle.

1 She lives in Spain. **Bai** / **Luci** / **Ivan** / **Ines**

2 He has a snake. **Bai** / **Luci** / **Ivan** / **Ines**

3 He doesn't like dogs. **Bai** / **Luci** / **Ivan** / **Ines**

4 She plays tennis. **Bai** / **Luci** / **Ivan** / **Ines**

5 He likes dancing. **Bai** / **Luci** / **Ivan** / **Ines**

6 She doesn't play sports. **Bai** / **Luci** / **Ivan** / **Ines**

7 He plays soccer. **Bai** / **Luci** / **Ivan** / **Ines**

8 She doesn't like snakes. **Bai** / **Luci** / **Ivan** / **Ines**

9 She has a cat. **Bai** / **Luci** / **Ivan** / **Ines**

✧ **Listen and check.** 52

✧ **Look again and complete.**

has	likes	lives	speaks

1 Bai .... in China.

2 Luci .... a dog.

3 Ivan .... Russian.

4 Ines .... painting.

1 Look, read and complete.

Melanie (1)..  in South Africa. She (2)..  Zulu and English. She (3).. ....  a pet. She (4)..  at seven o'clock. She goes to school at eight o'clock. She rides a (5)..  to school. She (6).. ....  sports. She (7)..  to bed at eight o'clock.

✧ **Listen and check.** 53

2 Unscramble.

1 He / in / India / lives ....

2 He / a pet parrot / has ....

3 doesn't / He / play / sports ....

4 He / singing / likes / and dancing. ....

✧ **Read, look and answer.**

What's his name? ....

1 Read the code and color.

languages = red countries = green

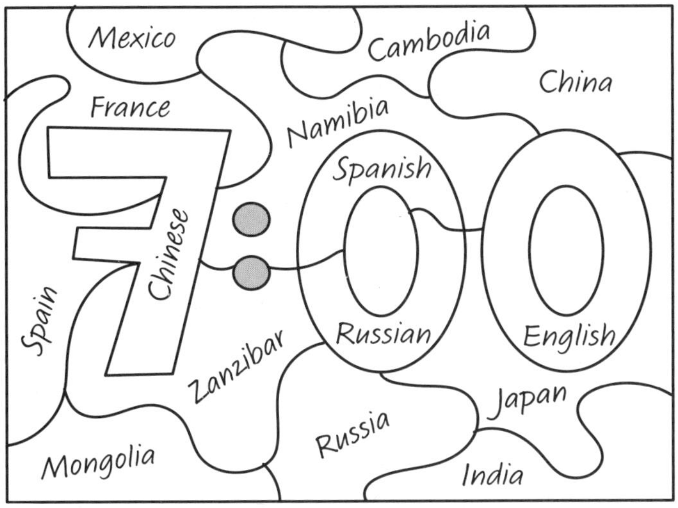

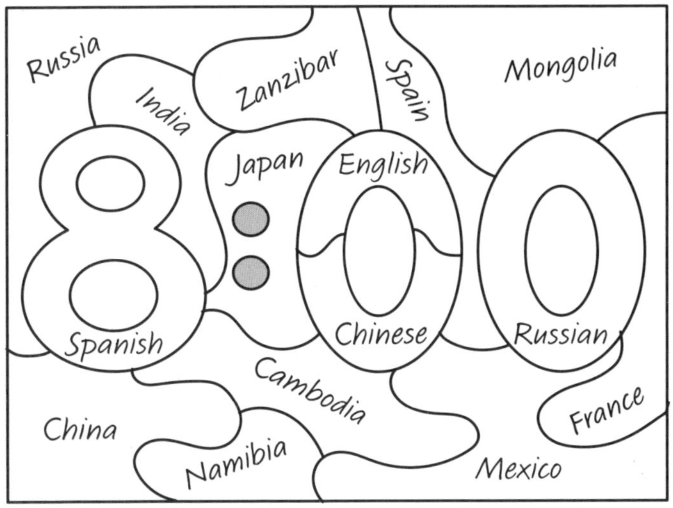

1 He wakes up at **six** / **seven** / **eight** o'clock.

2 He goes to bed at **six** / **seven** / **eight** o'clock.

✧ **Look and circle the times.**

2 Look and write the countries and languages.

Across: Countries

1

5

6

Down: Languages

2 ¡Hola!

3 Привет

4 你好

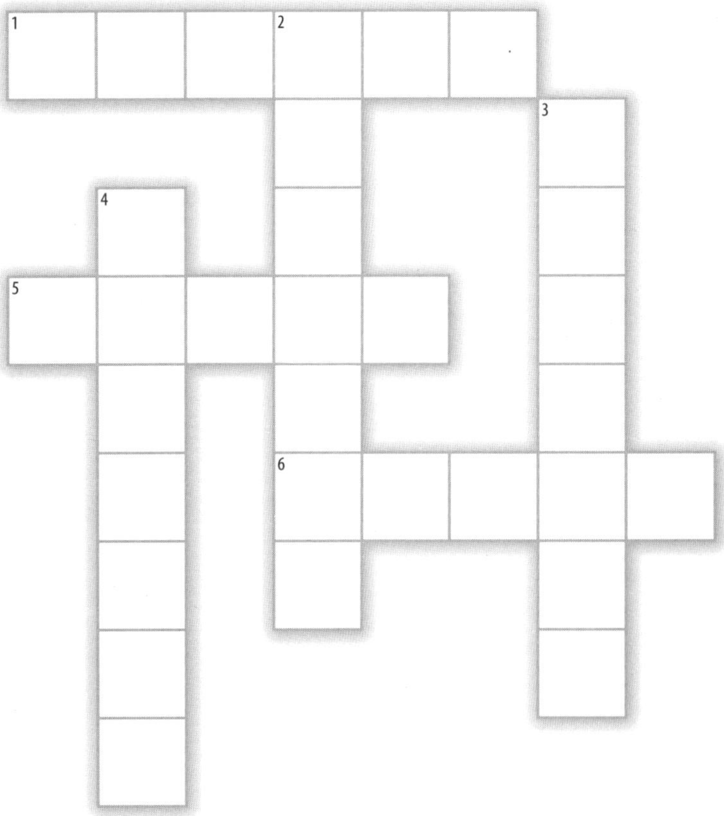

1 Look, read and circle.

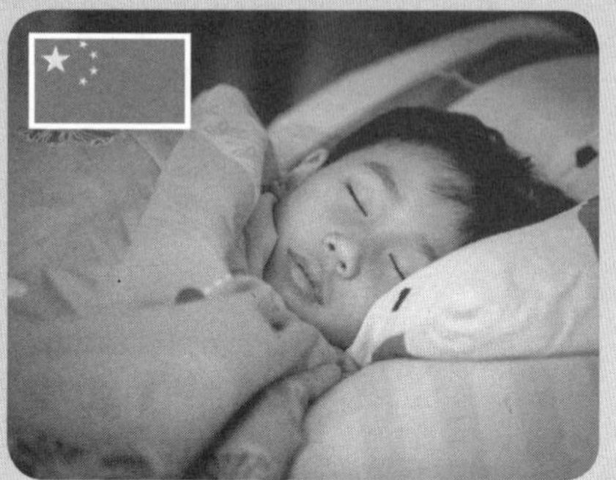

1 He lives in...

a China. b Russian. c English.

2 He ... at eight o'clock.

a goes to bed

b goes to school

c likes

3 He ... Chinese.

a lives b speaks c goes

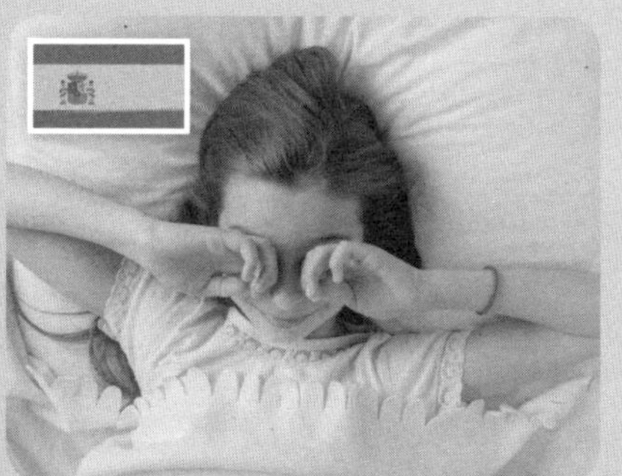

4 She ... at six o'clock.

a plays sports

b goes to school

c wakes up

5 She ... on a bike.

a wakes up b lives c goes to school

6 She speaks...

a China. b Spanish. c the USA.

7 She speaks...

a Russian. b China. c Russia.

8 She ... sports.

a doesn't like

b doesn't ride

c doesn't go

2 Read again and check your answers.

1 Write the times of day.

1

2

3

4

Times of Day

morning
afternoon
evening
night

Meals

breakfast
lunch
dinner

Routines

drink
eat
sleep

✧ Write the meals.

5

6

7

✧ Write the routines.

8

9

10
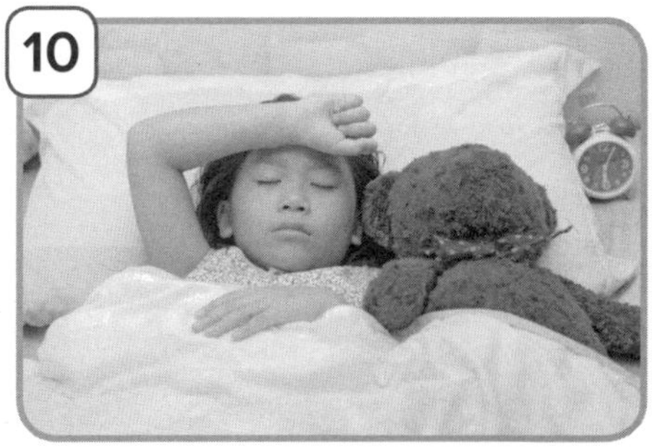

✧ Listen and check. 54

They eat breakfast.

They eat breakfast.
We don't wear shirts.

1 Look, read and circle.

1

They **eat** / **don't eat** lunch at school.

2

They **eat** / **don't eat** pizza for lunch.

3

They **drink** / **don't drink** milk at lunch.
They **drink** / **don't drink** juice.

4

They **wear** / **don't wear** a uniform at school.

5

They **sleep** / **don't sleep** on the school bus.

6

They **play** / **don't play** basketball at school.

Listen and check. 55

1 Read and match.

1 We eat breakfast...	at night.
2 We eat lunch...	in the morning.
3 We eat dinner...	in the evening.
4 We sleep...	in the afternoon.

✧ Look and match.

2 Circle about your school.

1 We **eat** / **don't eat** breakfast at school.

2 We **wear** / **don't wear** a school uniform.

3 We **play** / **don't play** sports at school.

4 We **sleep** / **don't sleep** in the classroom.

1 Look, read and match.

1

2

3

4

5
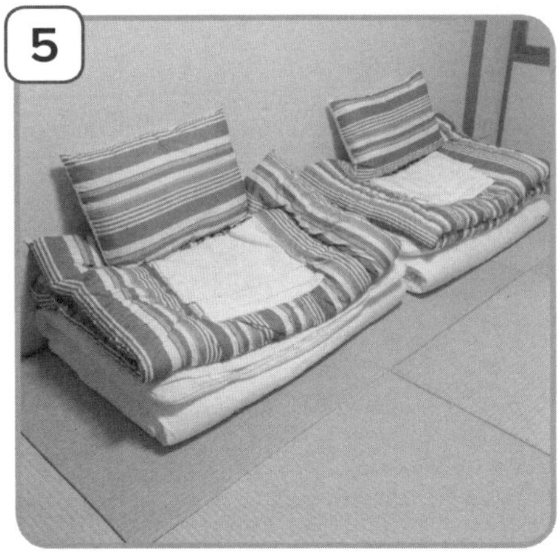
6

- [ ] In some houses in Japan, people don't sleep in a bed. They sleep on a mat.
- [ ] In the USA, people eat with a knife and fork. But they eat pizza with their hands.
- [ ] In some hot countries, children don't sleep in a bed. They sleep in a hammock.
- [ ] In many countries, people don't use a knife and fork. They eat with their hands.
- [ ] In this part of China, people don't live in houses. They live on boats.
- [ ] In some countries, people eat insects. Yum or yuck?

Listen and check. 56

1 Read and write.

1 We go to school on these days: ...., ..., ..., ..., ...

2 We don't go to school on these days: ...., ...

Days of the Week

Sunday
Monday
Tuesday
Wednesday
Thursday
Friday
Saturday

2 Look, read and complete.

don't eat   don't go   go   live   ride   sleep   wake up

Manuela and Laura live in Brazil. They (1)............................ at six o'clock in the morning. They (2)............................ .... to school on a bus. They go to school on a boat! At twelve o'clock, they go home. They (3)............................ in the afternoon for one or two hours. They go to bed at nine o'clock.

Jun and Fen (4)............................ in China. They (5)............................ their bikes to school. They go to school from eight o'clock in the morning until five o'clock in the afternoon! They (6)............................ .... lunch at home. They eat lunch at school. They eat dinner at home at six o'clock. They (7)............................ to bed at eight o'clock.

✧ **Listen and check.** 57

1 Read the clues and unscramble.

1 We eat this meal in the morning. karebstaf ....

2 We eat this meal in the afternoon. nulch ....

3 We eat this meal in the evening. ninder ....

4 We sleep at this time of the day. thing ....

5 We go to school at this time of day. gronnim ....

6 We go to bed at this time of day. givenen ....

7 We have lunch at this time of day. faretonno ....

2 Circle the seven days of the week.

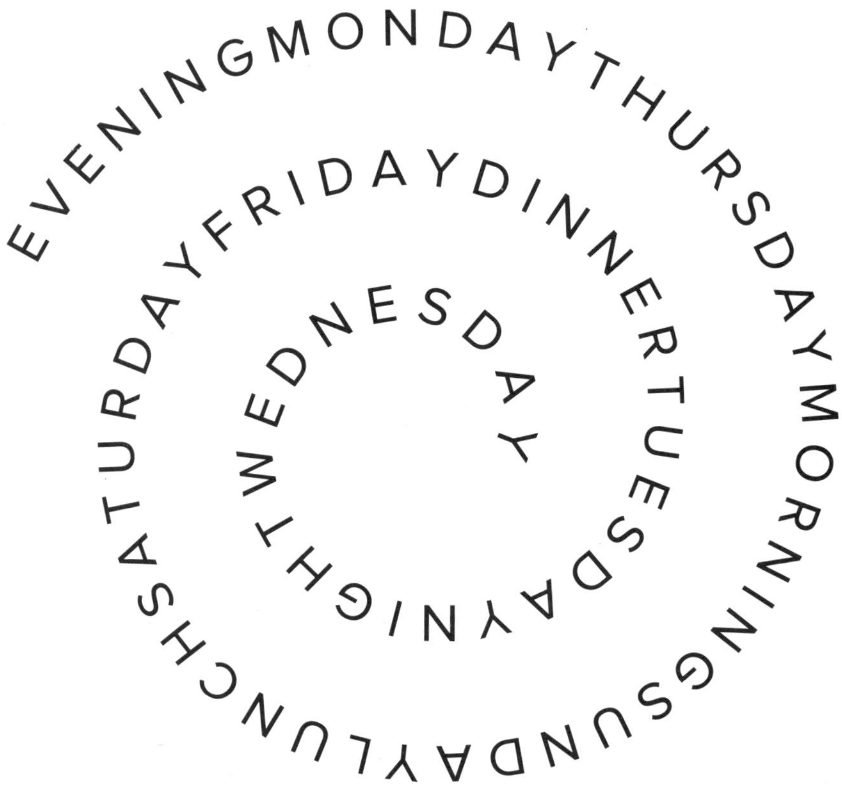

✧ Write the days in order.

1 S..............

2 ....

3 ....

4 ....

5 ....

6 ....

7 ....

1 Look, read and circle.

1 Time to wake up! It's six o'clock in the...

a morning. b afternoon. c night.

2 Time to go home! It's three o'clock in the...

a evening. b afternoon. c night.

3 We eat ... in the morning.

a lunch b dinner c breakfast

4 We eat ... in the afternoon.

a breakfast b dinner c lunch

5 We eat ... at night.

a dinner b lunch c breakfast

6 We go to bed and ... at nine o'clock at night.

a eat b drink c sleep

7 We ... pizza for breakfast.

a don't eat b don't drink c don't sleep

8 We ... juice for breakfast.

a eat b drink c sleep

2 Read again and check your answers.

Topic 8 Where do animals live?

Animals

crocodile
giraffe
hippo
lion
zebra

Nature

grass
river

Actions

hide
hunt

1 Label the animals.

1

Animal: ....

Habitat: **river** / **savanna**

Diet: **grass** / **fish**

Actions: sleep **in day** / **at night**

2

Animal: ....

Habitat: **river** / **savanna**

Diet: **grass** / **fish**

Actions: hunt **in day** / **at night**

3

Animal: ....

Habitat: **river** / **savanna**

Diet: **grass** / **animals**

Actions: hunt **in day** / **at night**

4

Animal: ....

Habitat: **river** / **savanna**

Diet: **grass** / **leaves**

Actions: **hide** / **hunt** in grass

5

Animal: ....

Habitat: **river** / **savanna**

Diet: **grass** / **leaves**

Actions: sleep **30 minutes** / **four hours** a day

Listen and check. Then circle the facts. 58

Does it hunt for food?

Does it hunt for food?
Yes, it does. / No, it doesn't.
Do they live in a savanna?
Yes, they do. / No, they don't.

1 Look, read and circle.

1

Do they hunt for food?

Yes, they do. / No, they don't.

Do they eat grass?

Yes, they do. / No, they don't.

2

Does it live in a savanna?

Yes, it does. / No, it doesn't.

Does it eat grass?

Yes, it does. / No, it doesn't.

3

Does the lion hunt the zebras?

Yes, it does. / No, it doesn't.

Do the zebras hide in the grass?

Yes, they do. / No, they don't.

✧ **Listen and check.** 59

1 Match.

1 Does a giraffe hide from zebras?

2 Do lions eat grass?

3 Does a crocodile hunt for food?

4 Do hippos live in rivers?

a No, they don't.

b Yes, it does.

c Yes, they do.

d No, it doesn't.

2 Look and circle.

1

Giraffes / **Zebras** eat leaves.

They live in a **savanna** / **river**.

2

Crocodiles live in a **river** / **savanna**.

They **hunt** / **hide from** fish.

3

Lions live in a **savanna** / **river**.

They **hunt** / **hide from** zebras.

4

Hippos live in a **savanna** / **river**.

They eat **grass** / **fish**.

Listen and check. 60

1 Read and match.

1 Does it live in a savanna? Yes, it does.

Does it eat grass? Yes, it does.

2 Does it live in a river? Yes, it does.

Does it eat grass? Yes, it does.

3 Does it live in a savanna? No, it doesn't.

Does it hunt? Yes, it does.

4 Does it live in a river? No, it doesn't.

Does it eat leaves? Yes, it does.

Listen and check. 61

Nature

leaf (pl. leaves)
tree

1 Look, read and complete.

leaves	trees

Giraffes eat .... at the top of ....

2 Read and color the correct animals.

1 This animal lives in a savanna. It hunts for food. It hides in long grass and hunts zebras and small giraffes. It can run fast, and it's loud!

2 These animals live in rivers. They swim or walk underwater! They don't hide from any animals. They're big! They eat grass. They can run fast.

Read again and answer the questions.

Yes, it does.	No, it doesn't.	Yes, they do.	No, they don't.

1 Does a lion live in a savanna? ....

2 Does it hunt hippos? ....

3 Do hippos hide from crocodiles? ....

4 Do they walk underwater? ....

1 Look and write the animals.

1
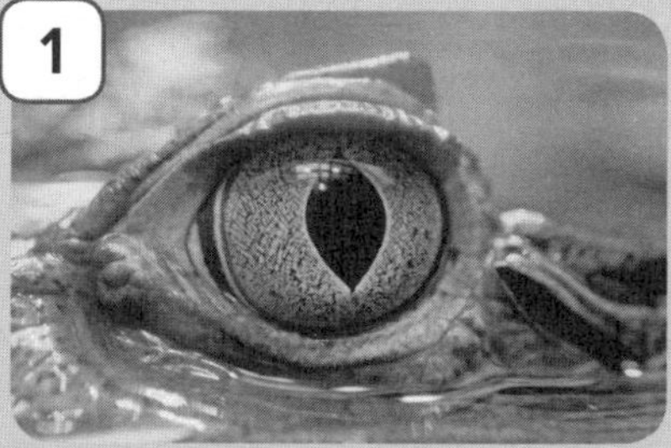
2
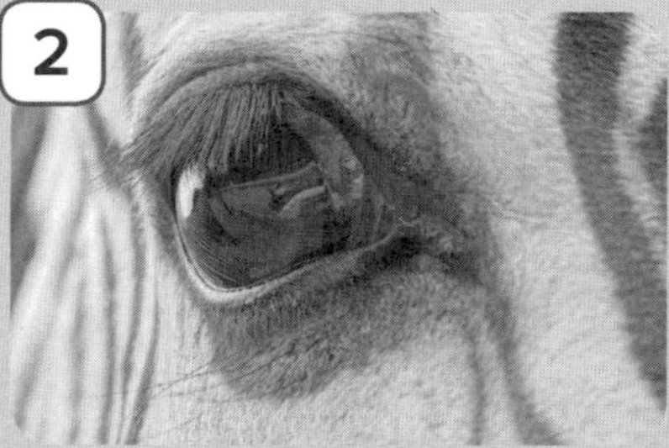
3
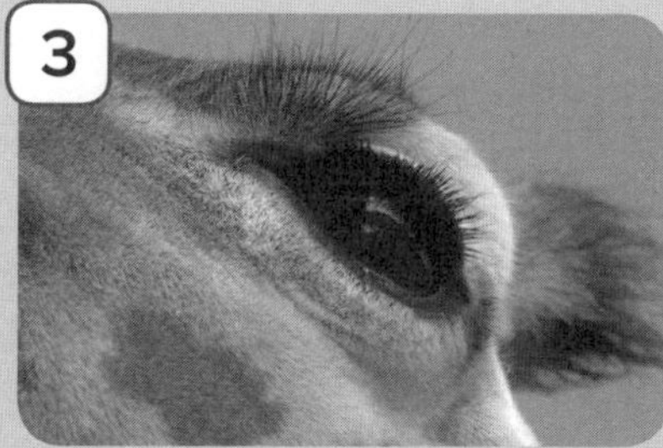

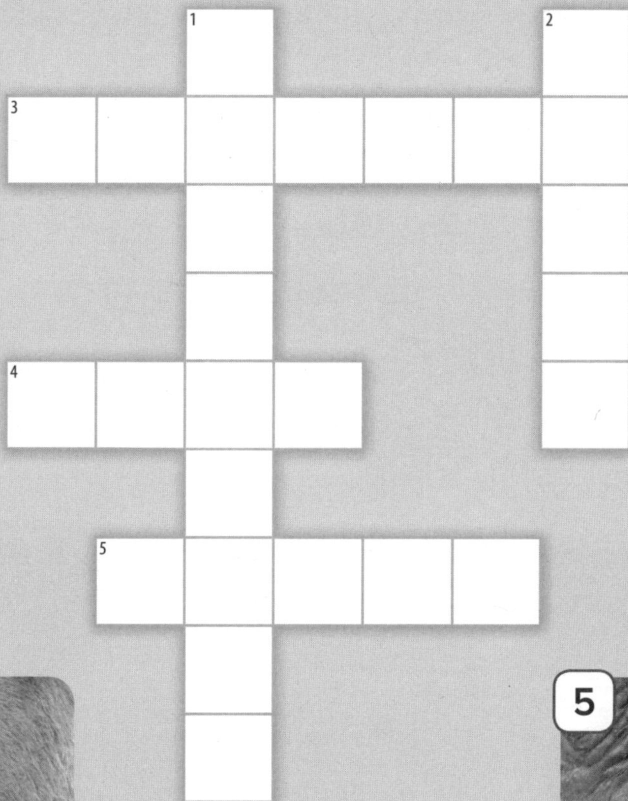

4
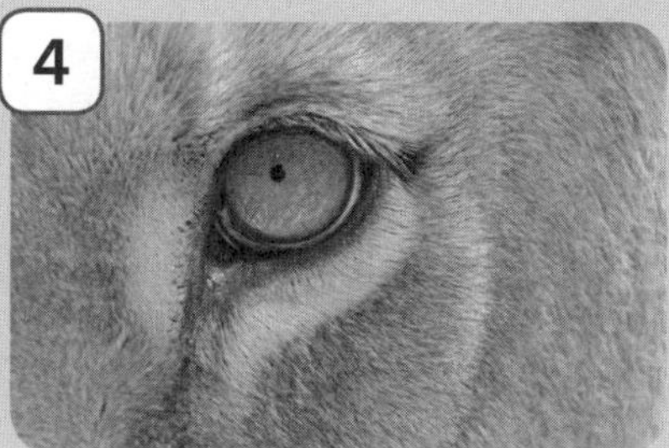
5

2 Circle nature words.

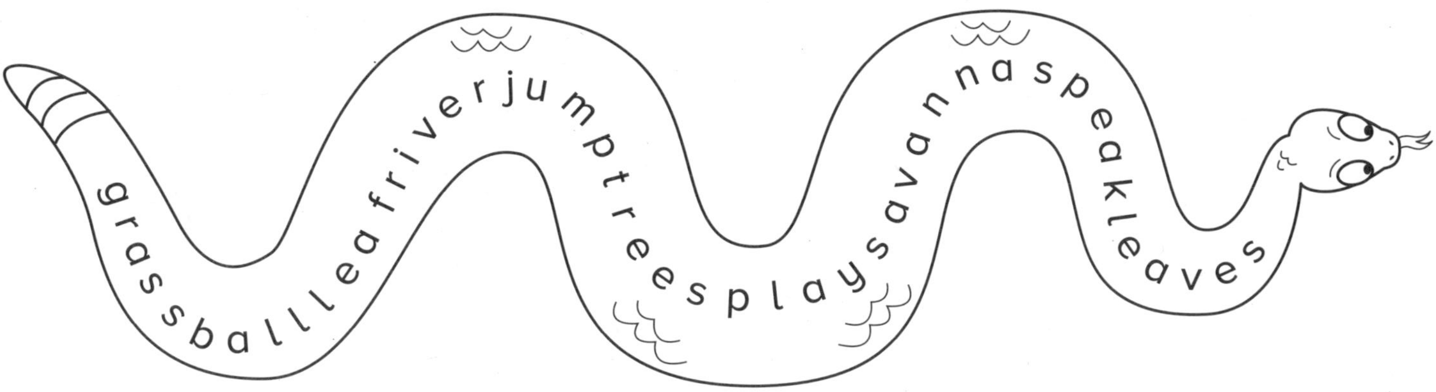

1 Look, read and circle.

1 This is a...

a giraffe. b crocodile. c zebra.

2 It ... fish and other animals.

a hides b hunts c lives

3 These are giraffes and...

a lions. b hippos. c zebras.

4 They live in...

a trees. b grass. c a savanna.

5 "... a lion hunt zebras?"

"Yes, it does."

a Does b Do c Is

6 "... the zebras run?"

"Yes, they do."

a Does b Do c Are

7 "Do hippos live in a river?"

"Yes, they..."

a don't. b doesn't. c do.

8 "Do they eat fish?

"No, they..."

a do. b don't. c does.

2 Read again and check your answers.

1 Complete with animals and nature words.

cave	forest	grass	tree

1

This .... is next to its ....

2

These .... are in a ....

3

This .... lives in a ....

4

These .... eat ....

5

These .... sleep in a ....

6

This .... sleeps in a ....

✧ **Listen and check.** 🔊62

Animals

bear
butterfly
(pl. butterflies)
deer (pl. deer)
mouse (pl. mice)
wolf (pl. wolves)

Nature

cave
forest

Where do they live?

Where do bears live? In the forest.
What do bears eat? They eat berries.
When do bears sleep? At night.
How do bears move? They walk and climb.

1 Match the questions with the answers.

1 Where do snakes sleep?
2 What do snakes eat?
3 When do snakes hunt?
4 How do snakes move?

a They slither. They can't walk or fly.
b They sleep in caves and trees.
c They eat small animals, like mice.
d Most snakes hunt at night.

✧ **Listen and check.** 63

✧ **Match with the pictures.**

1 Look, read and complete.

1

one wol............ two wol............

2

one d............ two d............

3

one m............ two m............

4

one butterfl............ two butterfl............

2 Read and write the question words.

How	What	When	Where

1 .... do butterflies move? They fly.

2 .... do mice sleep? They sleep in the day. They eat at night.

3 .... do wolves eat? They eat animals. They don't eat plants.

4 .... do deer live? They live in a forest.

✧ **Listen and check.** 64

✧ **Read again and match.**

1 Look and circle.

1 butterfly / butterflies 2 wolves / wolf 3 mouse / mice

Match the questions with the answers.

1 Where do they live? a They run.

2 What do they eat? b They hunt at night.

3 When do they hunt? c They eat meat.

4 How do they move? d They live in a forest.

Read again. Mark (✓) the correct animal.

Listen and check. 65

2 Unscramble and complete.

These .... a b e r s

live in a .... v e c a

in the .... r o f t e s

1 Look at the photos and read the answers. Complete the questions.

1 .... do bats sleep?

Bats sleep in caves and in trees.

2 .... do wolves

....................?

They hunt in a pack. They run after deer and other animals.

3 ....

bears ....?

Bears eat everything! They eat deer, fish, insects, grass and fruit.

4 ....

....?

Owls sleep in the day. They hunt at night.

1 Color the plural animals. Answer the question.

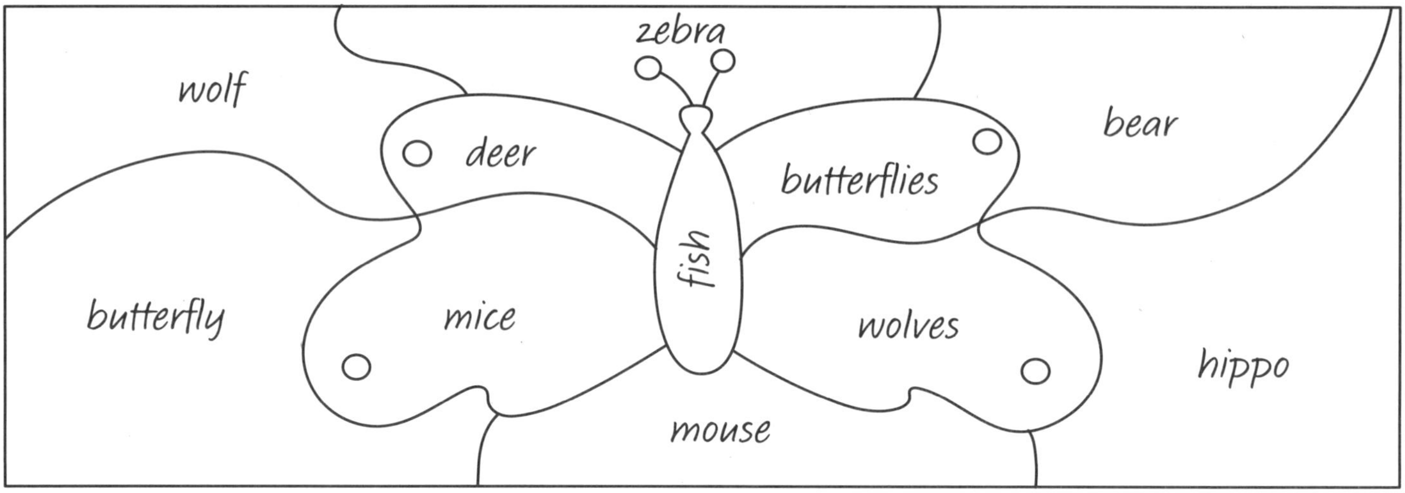

What animal is it? It's a ....

2 Circle four differences in picture B.

✦ Look and answer the questions.

caves climb fish grass night run trees

1 What do bears eat? They eat .... and ....

2 How do mice move? They .... and ....

3 Where do bats sleep? They sleep in .... and ....

4 When do owls hunt? They hunt at ....

1 Look, read and circle.

1 This is a pack of...

a deer. b wolves. c wolf.

2 "... do they live?"

"In a forest."

a Where b What c When

3 This is a...

a mice. b butterfly. c mouse.

4 "... does it sleep?"

"It sleeps in the day."

a What b When c How

5 This is a...

a bear. b deer. c wolf.

6 "... does it eat?"

"It eats grass."

a Where b How c What

7 This is a...

a bear. b bat. c wolf.

8 "... does it move?"

"It walks and runs."

a What b When c How

2 Read again and check your answers.

Topic 9 What's happening at home?

Actions

clean your room
do your homework
make breakfast
pick up toys
take a shower
use the computer
wash the dishes
watch TV

1 Label the pictures.

1

2

3

4

5

6

7

8

Listen and check. 66

2 Which do you do? Look and mark (✓ or ✗).

I'm cleaning my room.

I'm cleaning my room.
You're not helping.

1 Read, look and match.

☐ She's not washing the dishes. She's making breakfast.
☐ They're not watching TV. They're using the computer.
☐ She's not picking up toys. She's doing her homework.
☐ He's not cleaning his room. He's taking a shower.

1
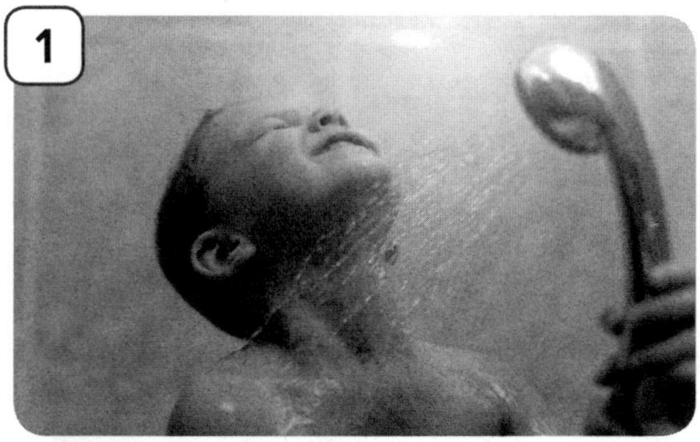

2

3

4

Listen and check. 67

2 Circle for you.

1 **I'm / I'm not** cleaning my room. 2 **I'm / I'm not** doing my homework.

1 Look and mark (✓ or ✗).

1

☐ I'm waking up.

2

☐ I'm watching TV.

3

☐ I'm cleaning my room.

4

☐ We're taking a shower.

5

☐ I'm washing a lettuce.

6

☐ I'm picking up toys.

✧ **Listen and check.** 🔊68

2 Match the verbs with the *–ing* forms.

use watch wash clean sleep take make swim run

washing sleeping taking running making

swimming watching cleaning using

1 Look and match.

1 clean
2 take
3 do
4 wash
5 make
6 watch
7 pick up
8 use

☐ the computer

☐ TV

☐ a shower

☐ toys

☐ your bedroom

☐ breakfast

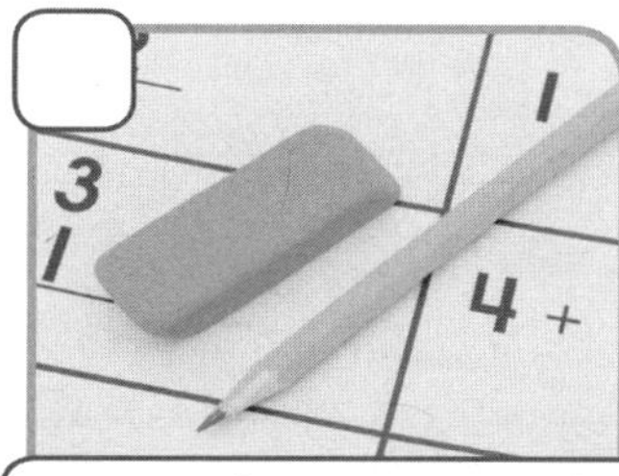

☐ your homework

☐ the dishes

2 Look, unscramble and complete.

1 toys / not / picking up / He's

....

He's .... books.

2 not / cleaning / She's / her desk

....

She's .... the board.

3 They're / watching TV / not

....

They're ....

4 not / He's / helping

....

He's ....

1 Label the clothes.

1 

2 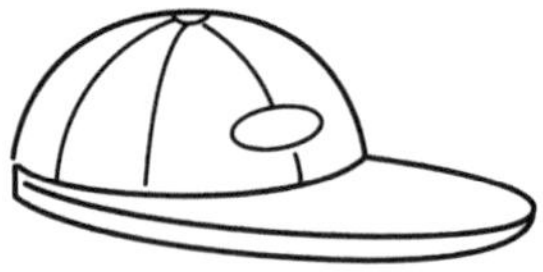

3 

4 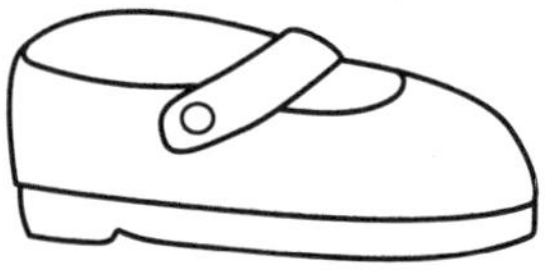

5 

6 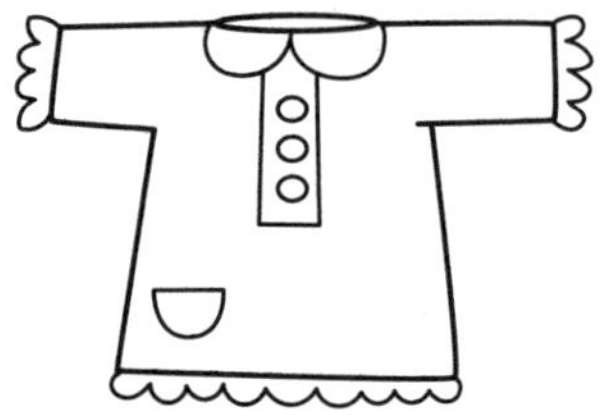

Clothing

dress
hat
pants
shirt
shoe
T-shirt

Actions

wear

✧ **Listen and color.** 69

2 Label the children and color their clothes.

1 Tom's wearing a red shirt and green pants. He's not wearing a hat.

2 Mike's wearing a blue T-shirt, orange pants and blue shoes. He's wearing a yellow hat.

3 Lynn's wearing a purple dress and yellow shoes. She's not wearing a hat.

4 Erin's wearing a red dress and black shoes. She's wearing a yellow hat.

a 

b 

c 

d 

1 Look, read and complete.

Across

3 The baby is ...

5 Kate and Cam are ... a cake.

6 Ben is ... toys.

8 Dad is ... a funny hat.

9 Dan is ... the dishes.

Down

1 Len is ... homework.

2 Mom is ... the table.

4 Tad and Eve are ... TV.

7 Lee and Toni are ... the computer.

1 Look, read and circle.

1 They're ... TV.

a watching   b washing   c using

2 She's wearing a...

a shoe.   b hat.   c dress.

3 He's not eating...

a breakfast.   b cereal.   c lunch.

4 He's wearing a...

a shirt.   b pants.   c T-shirt.

5 She's not ... the toys.

a picking up   b watching   c making

6 She's ... with them!

a taking   b cleaning   c playing

7 She's using the...

a computer.   b TV.   c dishes.

8 She's ... her homework.

a doing   b making   c taking

2 Read again and check your answers.

1 Look, read and match.

1

2

3

4

5
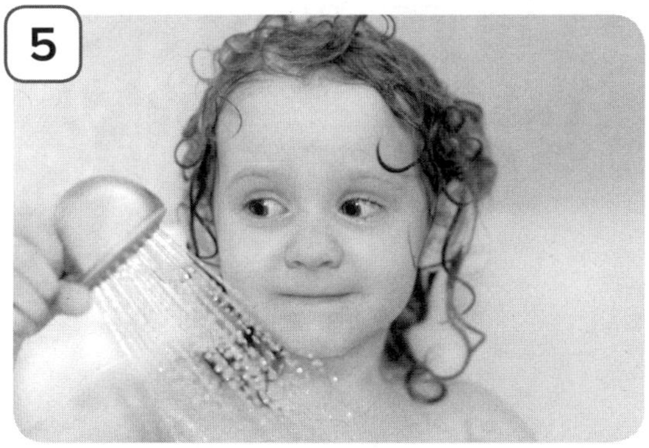

6

1 They're	working	in the yard.
2 He's	taking a shower	in the classroom.
3 They're	cooking	in the kitchen.
4 He's	sleeping	in the living room.
5 She's	eating an apple	in the bathroom.
6 She's	sitting on a sofa	in the bedroom.

✧ **Listen and check.** 70

Places at Home

bedroom
kitchen
living room
yard

Furniture

sofa

Actions

cook
sit
work

Are you eating?

Are you **eating**?
Yes, I **am**. / No, I**'m not**.
What **are** you **doing**?
I**'m cooking**.

1 Look, read and circle.

1

What's **she** / **he** doing?

She's / **I'm** sleeping.

2

What **are** / **is** they doing?

They're **working** / **sleeping** in the yard.

3

What's / **What** she doing?

She's cooking.

Is she / **She is** making breakfast?

No, she isn't.

4

What's he **doing** / **eating**?

He's watching a movie.

Is he / **He is** eating popcorn?

Yes, he is.

Listen and check. 71

1 Label the places at home.

1

....

2

....

3

....

4

....

✧ Look, read and complete.

am are I'm we We're What you

1 What are you doing?

.... watching TV.

Are you eating snacks?

Yes, ... are.

2 What are .... doing?

I'm cooking.

Are you making breakfast?

Yes, I ....

3 .... are you doing?

.... working.

Are you doing your homework?

Yes, I am.

4 What .... you doing?

I'm working.

Are .... washing the car?

Yes, I am.

1 Look and write the places at home.

1

What's happening in the ....?

2

What's happening in the ....?

3

What's happening in the ....?

✧ Match the questions with the answers.

☐ The dog's hiding under the bed.

☐ Grandpa's working on the computer.

☐ Grandma's riding her bike.

2 Look, read and unscramble.

1

Are you doing your homework?
No, I'm not.

....
....

The / books / on / sleeping / my / cat's

2

Are you watching TV?
No, I'm not.

....
....

bedroom / I'm / in / reading / my

3

Is Karl playing in his bedroom?
No, he isn't.

....
....

yard / He's / in / hiding / the

✧ Listen and check. 🔊72

1 Match the questions with the pictures.

1 What are Dad and the baby doing in the yard?

2 Is your brother sleeping in the bedroom?

3 Is Mom playing with the dog?

4 Is Grandfather reading in the living room?

☐ No, she isn't.

She's .... the kitchen.

☐ They're ....

a shower.

☐ No, he isn't.

He's ....

☐ No, he isn't.

He's .... on the bed.

✧ **Complete the answers.**

cleaning jumping sleeping taking

✧ **Listen and check.** 🔊73

1 Match the actions with the people.

☐ taking a shower	☐ using the computer	☐ sleeping
☐ making breakfast	☐ washing the dishes	☐ sitting on the sofa
☐ watching TV	☐ cooking	

2 Look and complete the words.

1 We're .....[4] ..... o.....[1] .... lunch.

2 We're s.....tt.....[2] .....[6]g in the yard.

3 The dog's .....[5]a.....[3] .....n..... our meat!

✦ **What's Mom doing?**

Write the hidden word.

She's hiding in the

.....[1] .....[2] .....[3] .....[4] h .....[5] .....[6]!

1 Look, read and circle.

1 "Where are they?" "They're in the..."

a kitchen. b bedroom. c yard.

2 "... they working?" "No, they aren't."

a Are b Is c What

3 "Where are they?" "They're in the..."

a kitchen. b bathroom. c living room.

4 "Are they ... on the sofa?" "Yes, they are."

a cooking b sitting c working

5 "Where is she?" "She's in the..."

a kitchen. b bathroom. c bedroom.

6 "... cooking?" "No, she isn't."

a Is she b She's c She is

7 "... happening?" "We're watching a movie."

a What b What's c Where's

8 "... you eating popcorn?" "No, we aren't."

a Is b Are c Do

2 Read again and check your answers.

Richmond
58 St Aldates
Oxford
OX1 1ST
United Kingdom

First Edition: 2019
ISBN: 978-607-06-1599-3

Compass Vocabulary and Grammar Log
Starter Level

Av. Río Mixcoac No. 274, Col. Acacias,
Del. Benito Juárez, C.P. 03240, Ciudad de México

Text: Alex Mackenzie

Publisher: Justine Piekarowicz
Project Manager: Amanda Guppy
Editor: Dominic Wright
Design: Orlando Llanas, Erika Martínez
Layout: Jaime Angeles, Karen Esquivel
Cover Photograph: © Gettyimages.com: Maria Kovalevskaya

Illustrations: María Guadalupe Calvo Leyva pp. 3, 5, 10, 13, 17, 18, 19, 20, 21, 23, 24, 27, 30, 31, 32, 34, 35, 38, 39, 40, 42, 45, 47, 49, 52, 54, 55, 58, 59, 61, 63, 66, 68, 73, 76, 77, 79, 80, 81, 84, 87, 89, 90, 91, 94, 101, 104, 108, 112, 115, 117, 118, 119, 122, 124, 126; Pablo Sebastián Pino pp. 9, 10, 12, 13, 14

Photographs: © **Depositphotos.com:** OlegDoroshenko p. 28 (last picture), krailurkA p. 79 (seventh picture), pftrip p. 81 (first picture), imagex p. 96 (second picture), CatherineL-Prod p. 96 (fourth picture), jeffcagle p. 96 (sixth picture), Lazyllama p. 97 (first picture), Baiterek_Media p. 97 (second picture); © **Gettyimages.com:** Danny Iacob (back cover)

Images used under license from © **Depositphotos.com**, © **Shutterstock.com**, © **Stock.adobe.com**

Printed in Mexico by

Corporativo Prográfico S.A de C.V.
Calle Dos Núm. 257, Bodega 4, Col Granjas San Antonio
C.P. 09070 Del. Iztapalapa, Mexico, Mexico city.
in Jun 2019.